Lizzie McGUiRE

Volume 6

Series created by Terri Minsky

"Movin' On Up"

written by Nina G. Bargiel & Jeremy J. Bargiel

"Mom's Best Friend"

written by Douglas Tuber & Tim Maile

Contributing Editors - Robert Buscemi & Amy Court Kaemon
Layout & Lettering - Yolanda Petriz
Cover Layout - Patrick Hook
Graphic Designer & Additional Layout - Tomás Montalvo-Lagos &
Jennifer Nunn-Iwai

Editors - Elizabeth Hurchalla & Jod Kaftan
Digital Imaging Manager - Chris Buford
Pre-Press Manager - Antonio DePietro
Production Managers - Jennifer Miller, Mutsumi Miyazaki
Art Director - Matt Alford
Managing Editor - Jill Freshney
VP of Production - Ron Klamert
President & C.O.O. - John Parker
Publisher & C.E.O. - Stuart Levy

Come visit us online at www.TOKYOPOP.com

A ⊚TOKYOPOP® Cine-Manga™
TOKYOPOP Inc.
5900 Wilshire Blvd., Suite 2000, Los Angeles, CA 90036

LIZZIE MCGUIRE VOLUME 6

© 2004 Disney Enterprises, Inc.

ISBN: 1-59182-572-5

First TOKYOPOP printing: June 2004

10 9 8 7 6 5 4 3 2 1

Printed in China

LIZZIE McGUIRE

Volume 6

CONTENTS

Lizzie McGuire

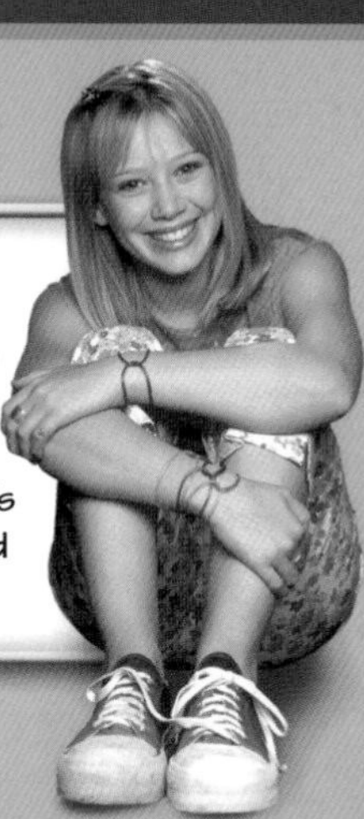

LIZZIE MCGUIRE:
A typical 14-year-old girl who has her fair share of bad hair days and embarrassing moments. Luckily, Lizzie knows how to admit when she's wrong, back up her friends and stand up for herself.

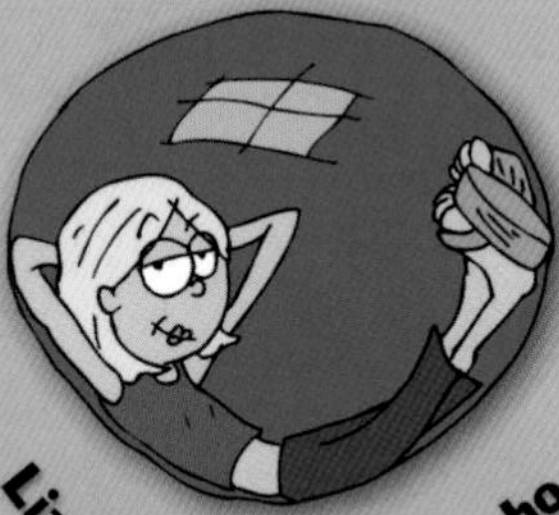

Lizzie's alter-ego, who says and does all the things Lizzie's afraid to.

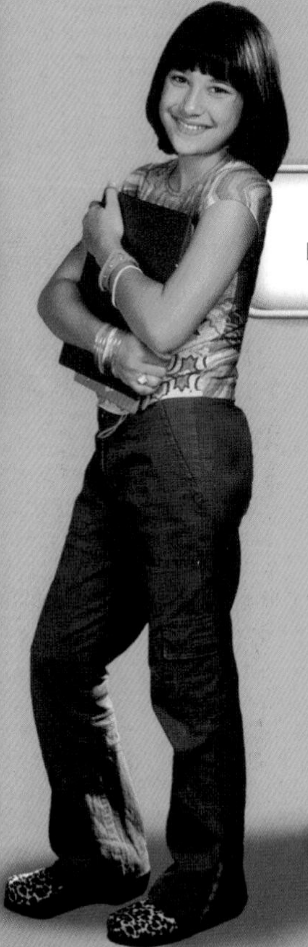

MIRANDA:
Lizzie's best friend.

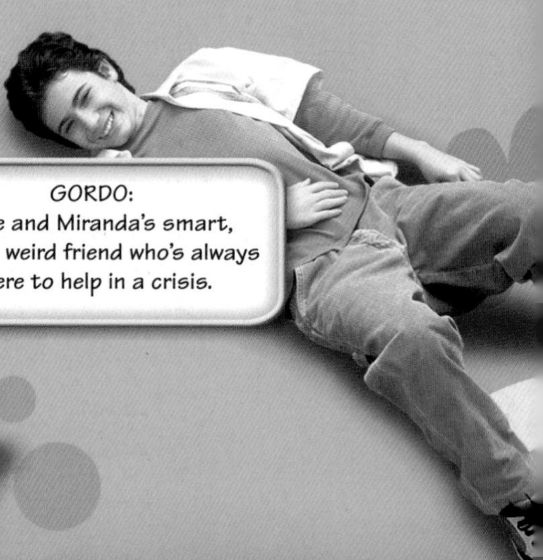

GORDO:
Lizzie and Miranda's smart, slightly weird friend who's always there to help in a crisis.

CHARACTER BIOS

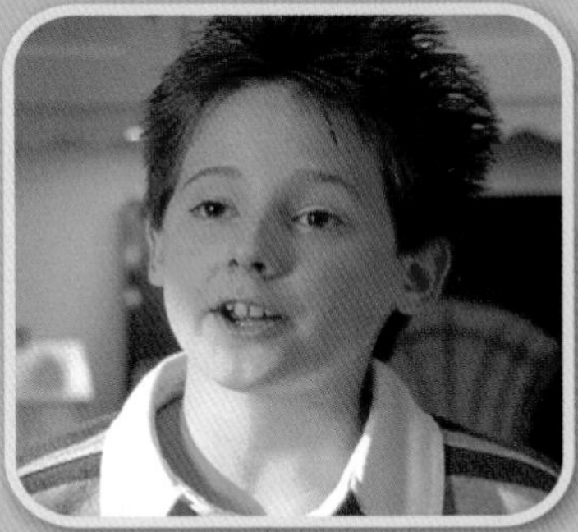

MATT:
Lizzie's little brother, who spends most of his time driving her crazy.

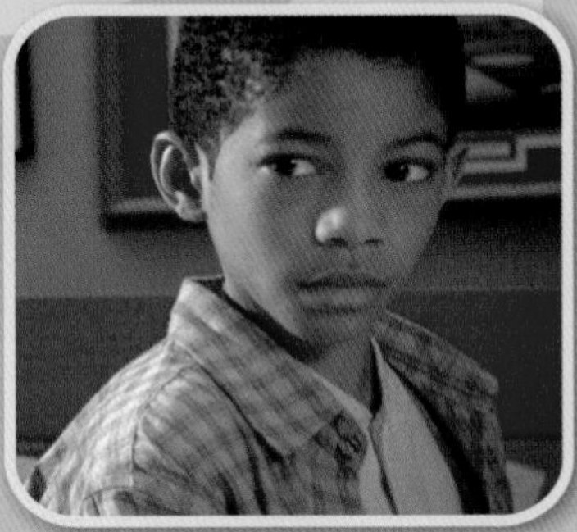

LANNY:
Matt's best friend.

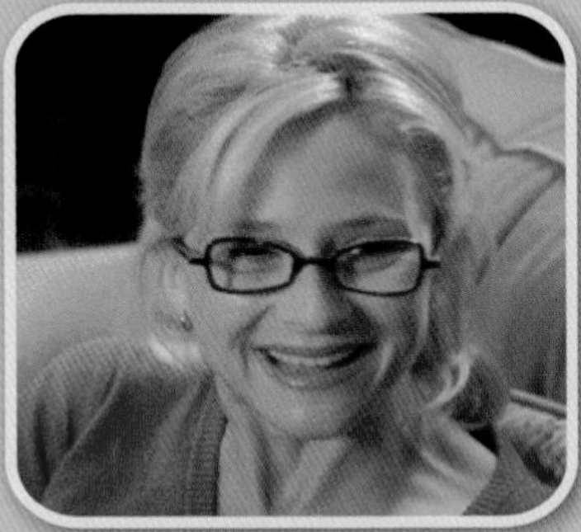

LIZZIE'S MOM:
She only wants the best for Lizzie, but sometimes she tries a little too hard.

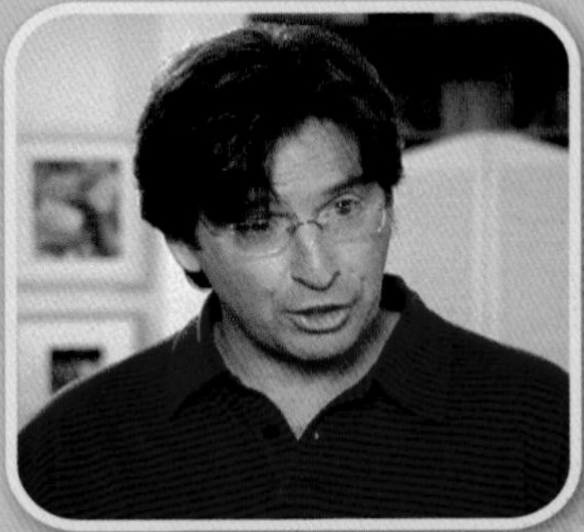

LIZZIE'S DAD:
He loves Lizzie, though he doesn't always know how to relate to her.

Lizzie McGuire

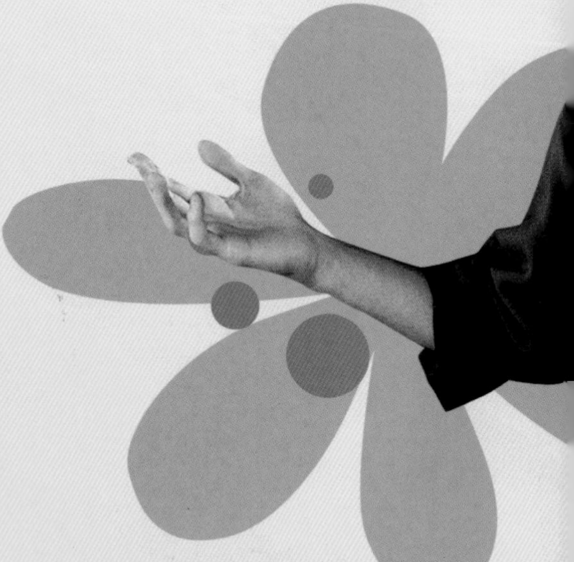

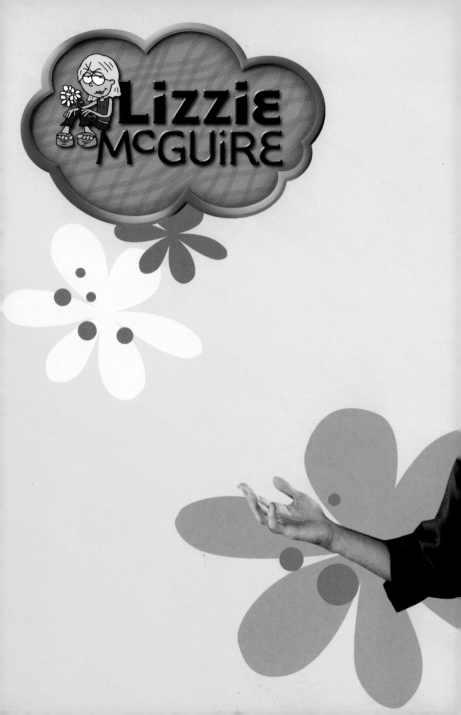

Episode 11

"Movin' On Up"

Gordo jumps at the chance to skip eighth grade and head to high school. At first the girls are excited for him—high school's just so much cooler than middle school. But when reality sets in, Lizzie goes from impressed to depressed. With Gordo gone, will things ever be the same for the three friends? And why does Lizzie miss him as much as she does?

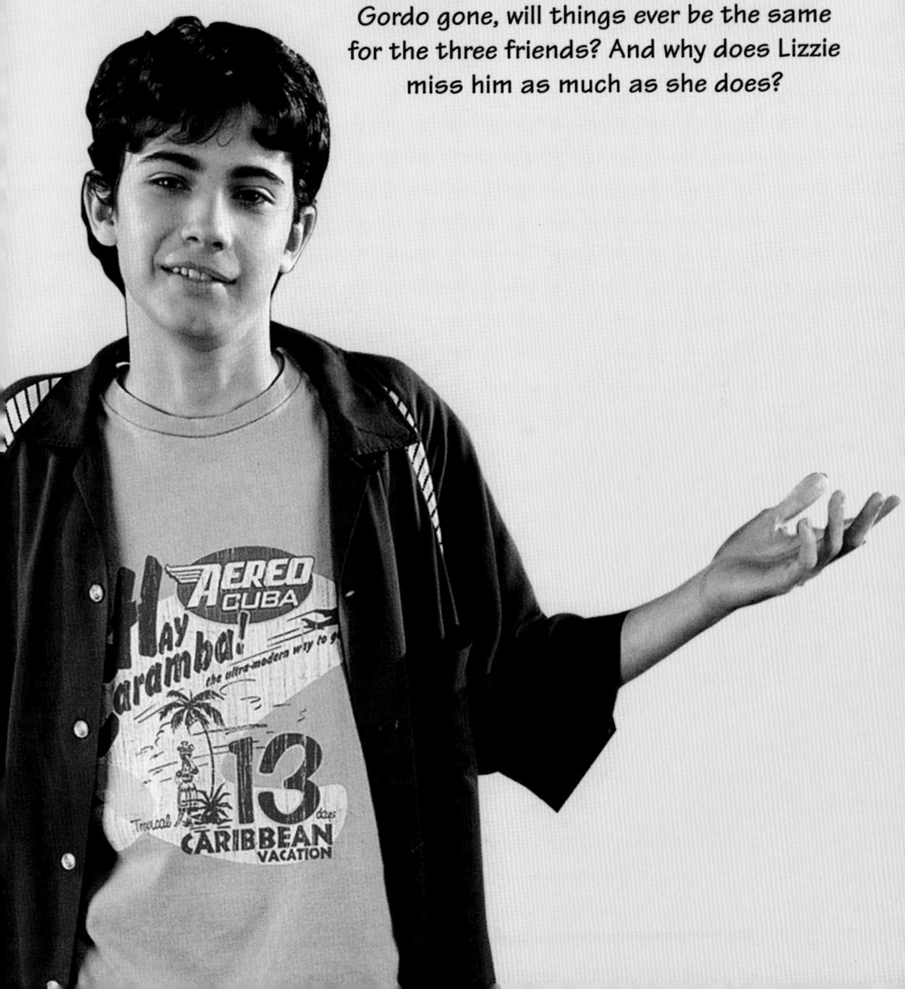
AEREO
CUBA
13
CARIBBEAN
VACATION

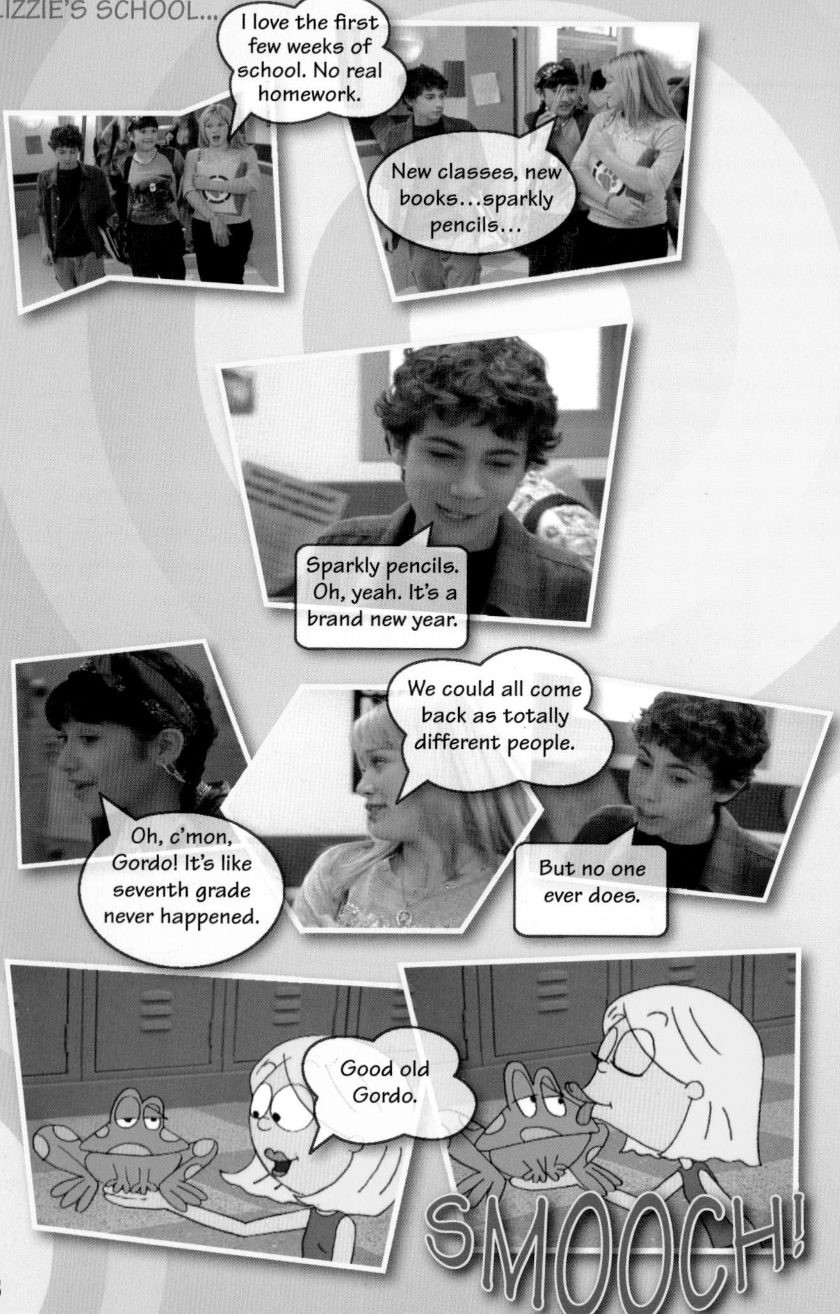
I love the first few weeks of school. No real homework.
New classes, new books...sparkly pencils...
Sparkly pencils. Oh, yeah. It's a brand new year.
Oh, c'mon, Gordo! It's like seventh grade never happened.
We could all come back as totally different people.
But no one ever does.
Good old Gordo.
SMOOCH!

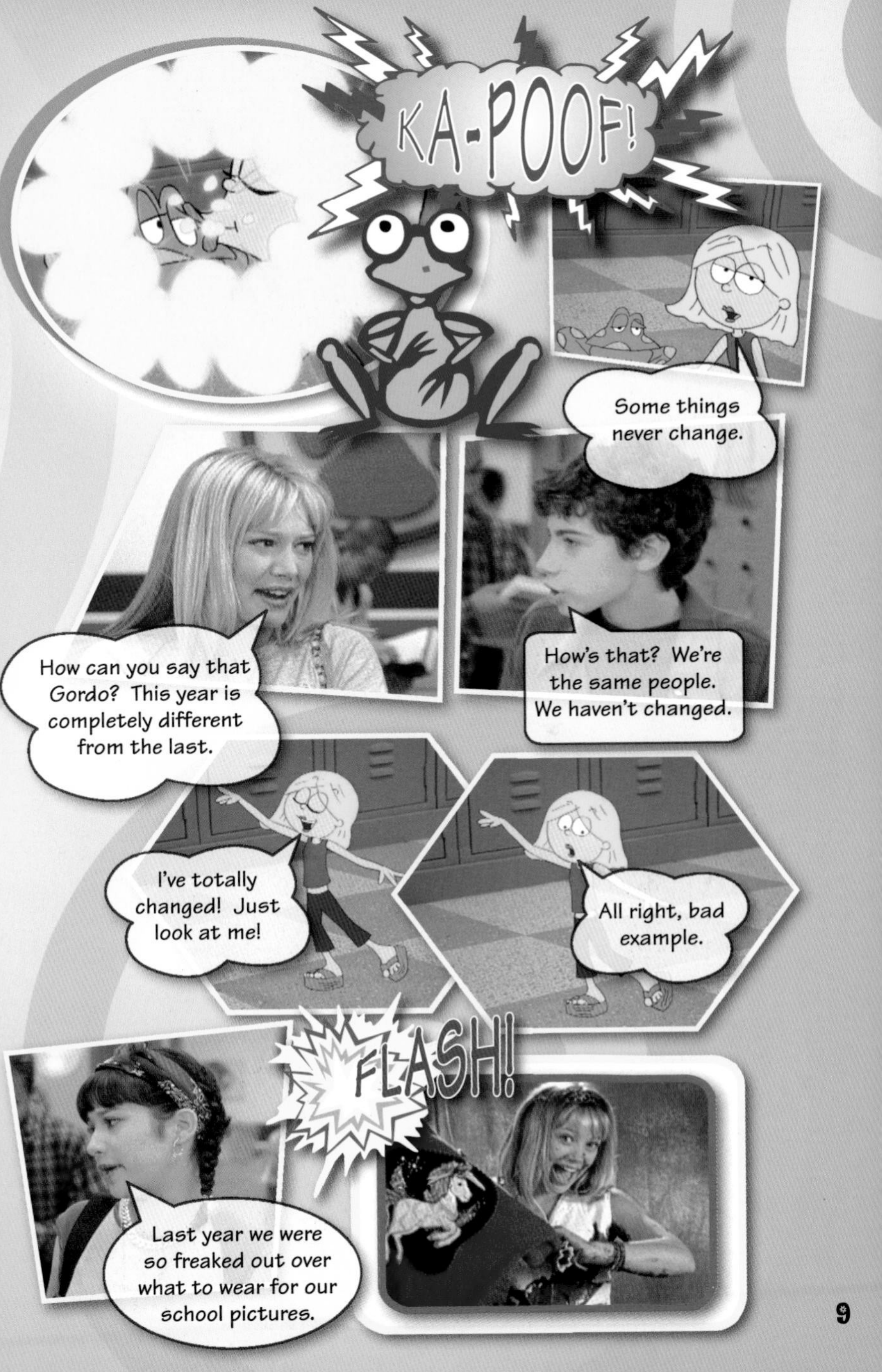
KA-POOF!
Some things never change.
How can you say that Gordo? This year is completely different from the last.
How's that? We're the same people. We haven't changed.
I've totally changed! Just look at me!
All right, bad example.
FLASH!
Last year we were so freaked out over what to wear for our school pictures.

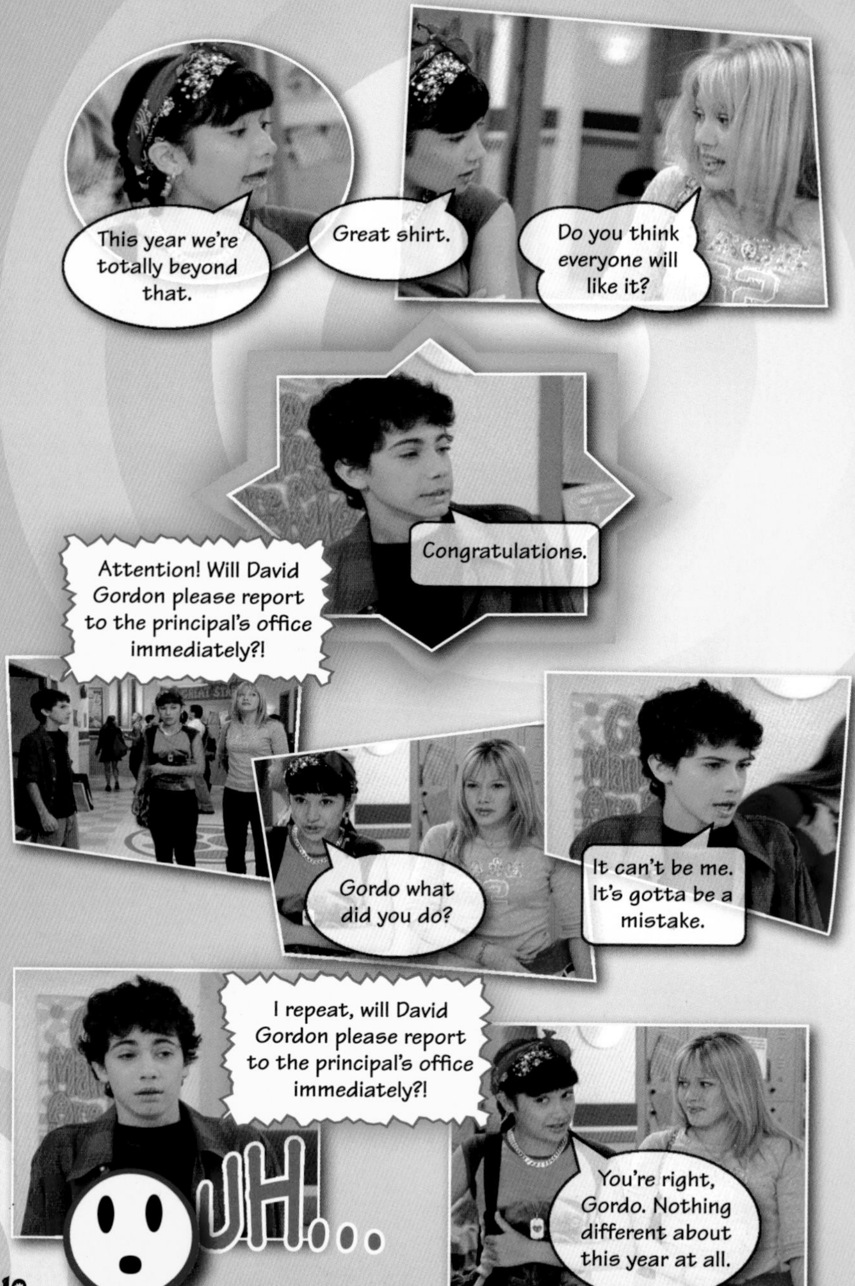
This year we're totally beyond that.
Great shirt.
Do you think everyone will like it?
Congratulations.
Attention! Will David Gordon please report to the principal's office immediately?!
Gordo what did you do?
It can't be me. It's gotta be a mistake.
I repeat, will David Gordon please report to the principal's office immediately?!
UH...
You're right, Gordo. Nothing different about this year at all.

AT LUNCH...

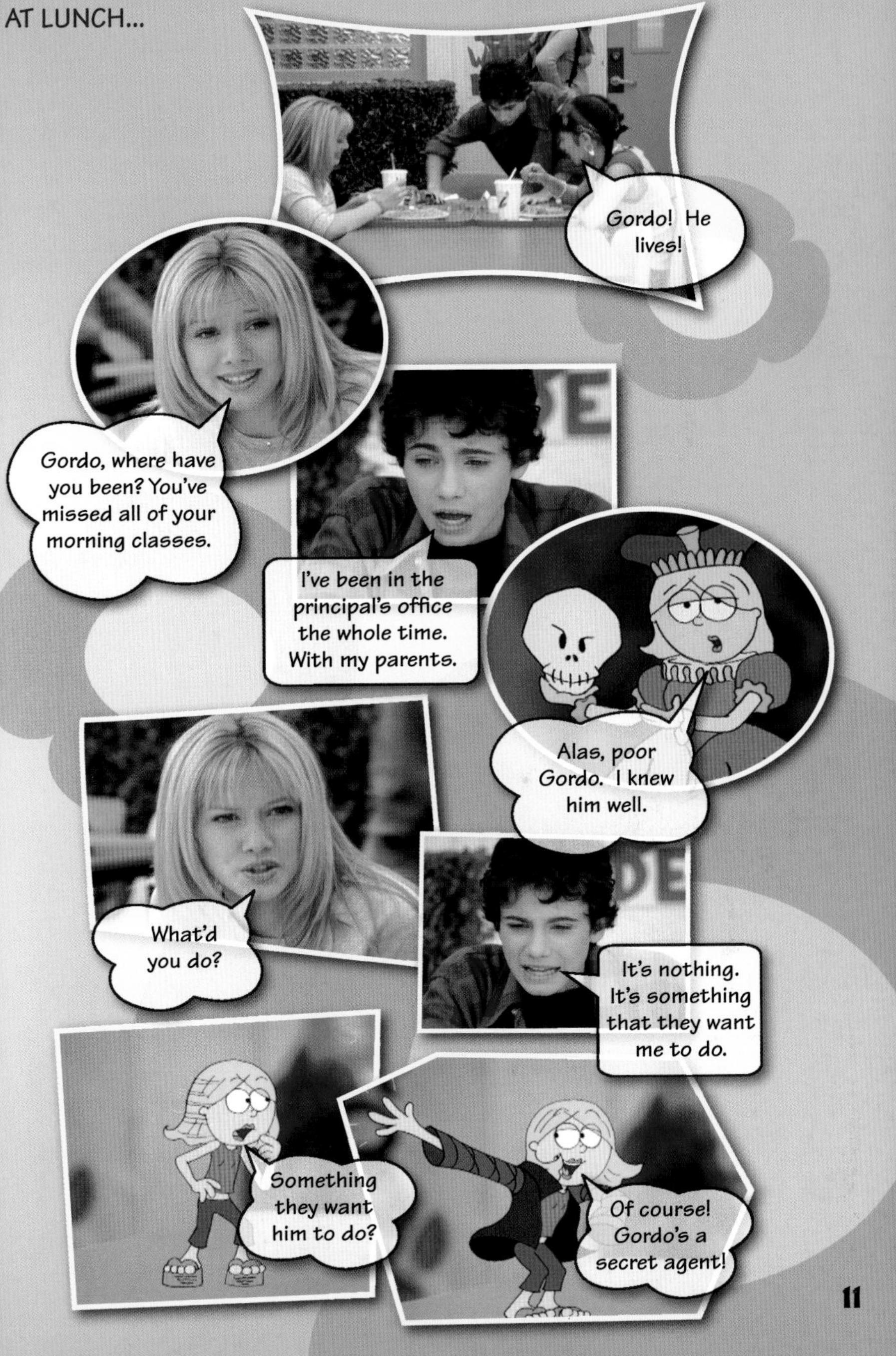
Gordo! He lives!
Gordo, where have you been? You've missed all of your morning classes.
I've been in the principal's office the whole time. With my parents.
Alas, poor Gordo. I knew him well.
What'd you do?
It's nothing. It's something that they want me to do.
Something they want him to do?
Of course! Gordo's a secret agent!

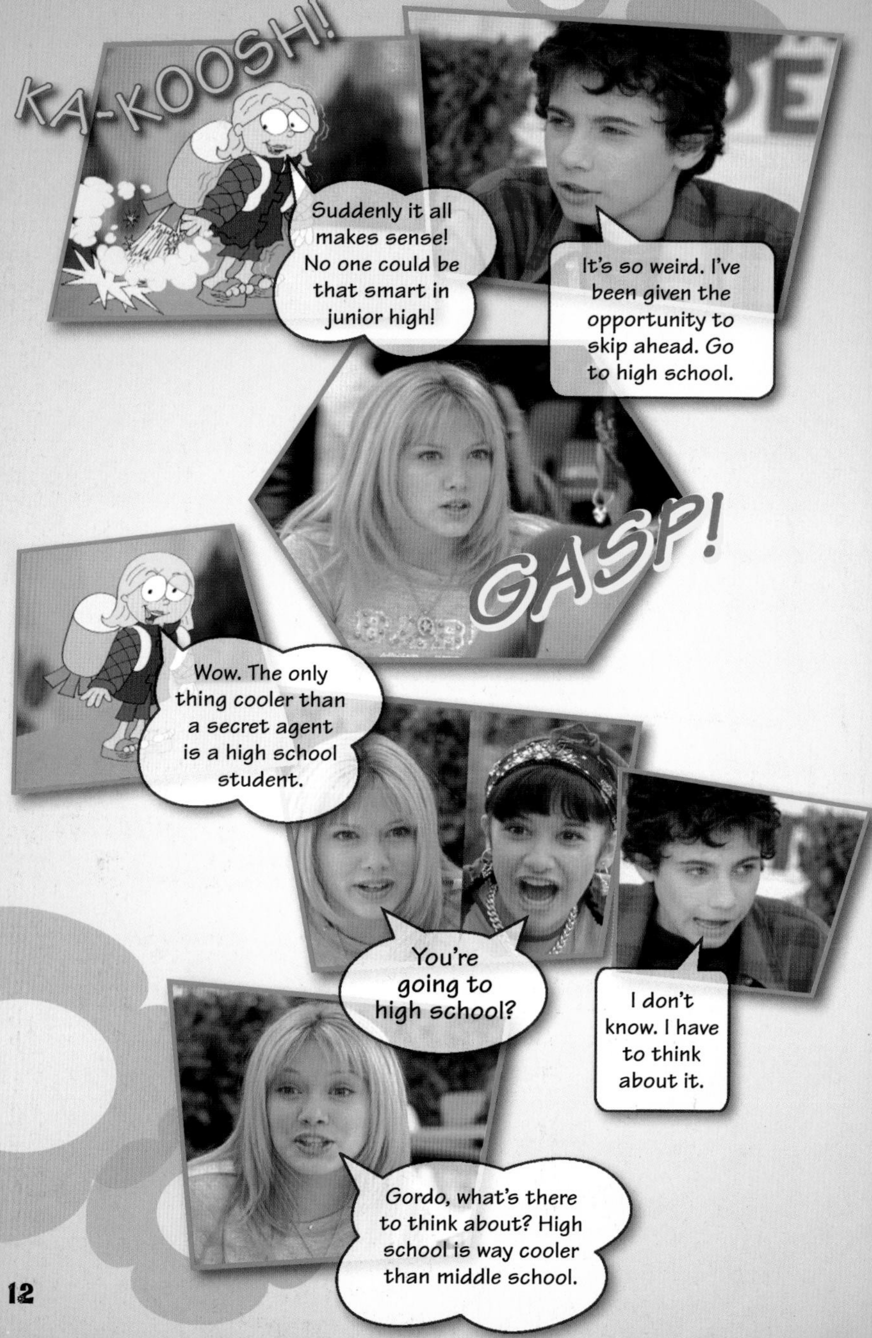
KA-KOOSH!
Suddenly it all makes sense! No one could be that smart in junior high!
It's so weird. I've been given the opportunity to skip ahead. Go to high school.
GASP!
Wow. The only thing cooler than a secret agent is a high school student.
You're going to high school?
I don't know. I have to think about it.
Gordo, what's there to think about? High school is way cooler than middle school.

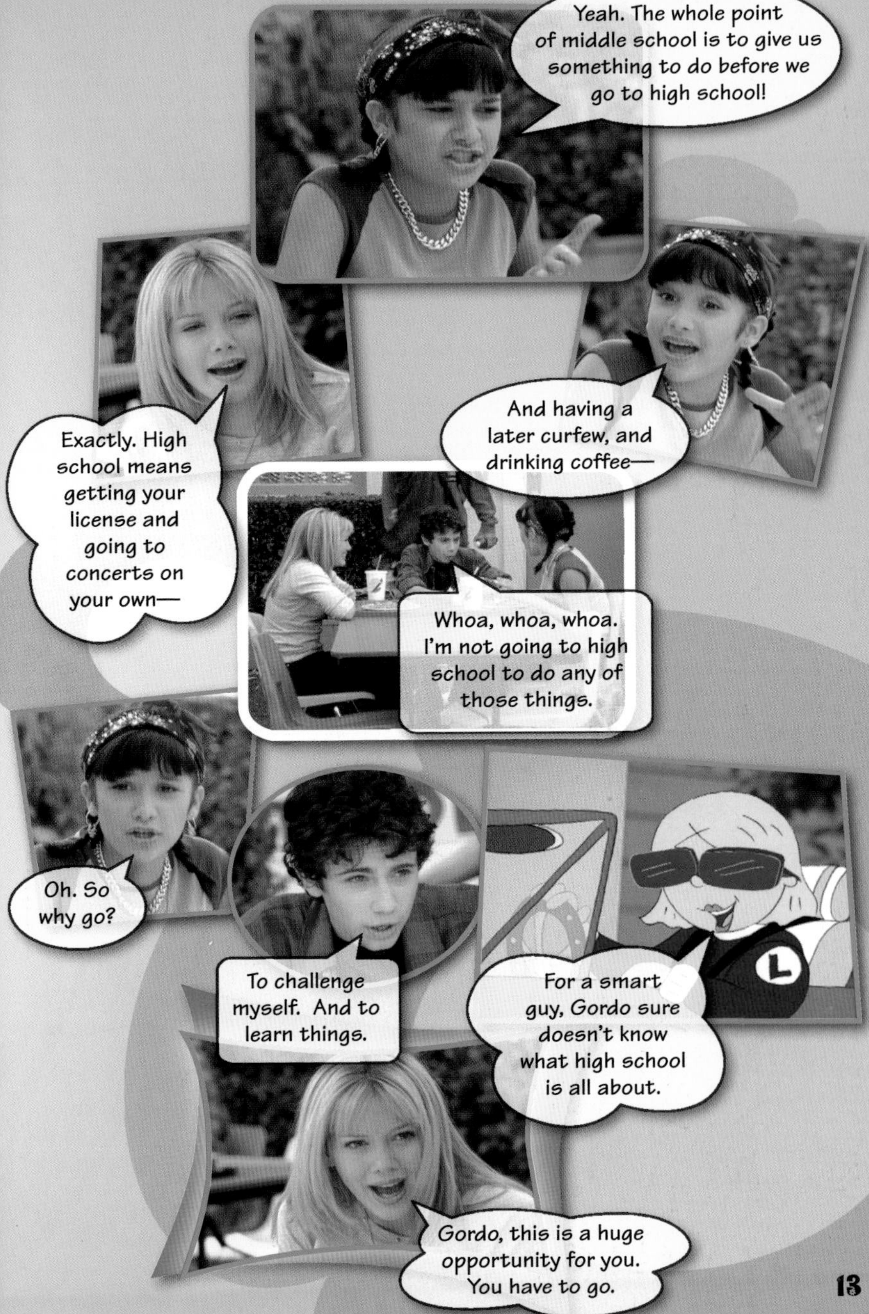
Yeah. The whole point of middle school is to give us something to do before we go to high school!
Exactly. High school means getting your license and going to concerts on your own—
And having a later curfew, and drinking coffee—
Whoa, whoa, whoa. I'm not going to high school to do any of those things.
Oh. So why go?
To challenge myself. And to learn things.
For a smart guy, Gordo sure doesn't know what high school is all about.
Gordo, this is a huge opportunity for you. You have to go.

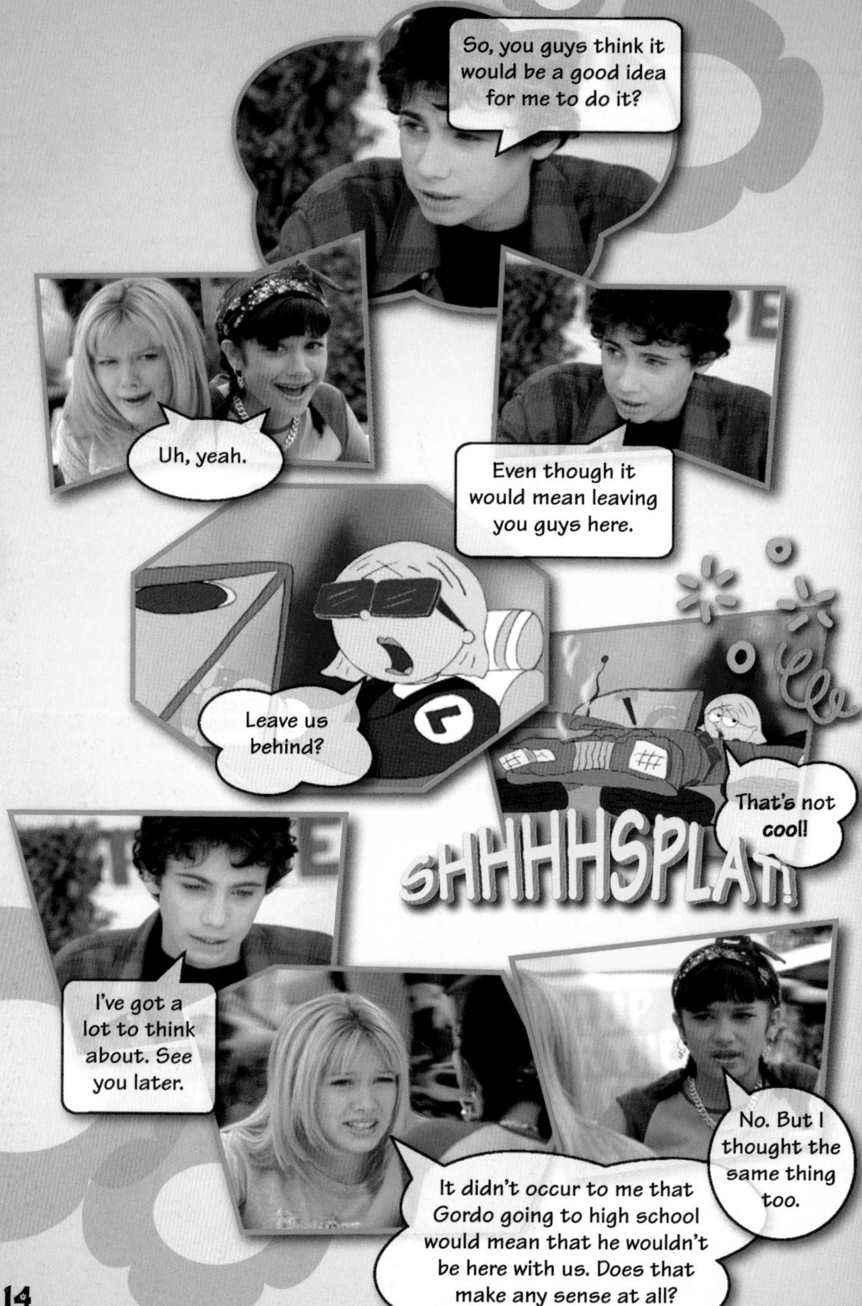
So, you guys think it would be a good idea for me to do it?
Uh, yeah.
Even though it would mean leaving you guys here.
Leave us behind?
That's not cool!
SHHHHSPLAT!
I've got a lot to think about. See you later.
It didn't occur to me that Gordo going to high school would mean that he wouldn't be here with us. Does that make any sense at all?
No. But I thought the same thing too.

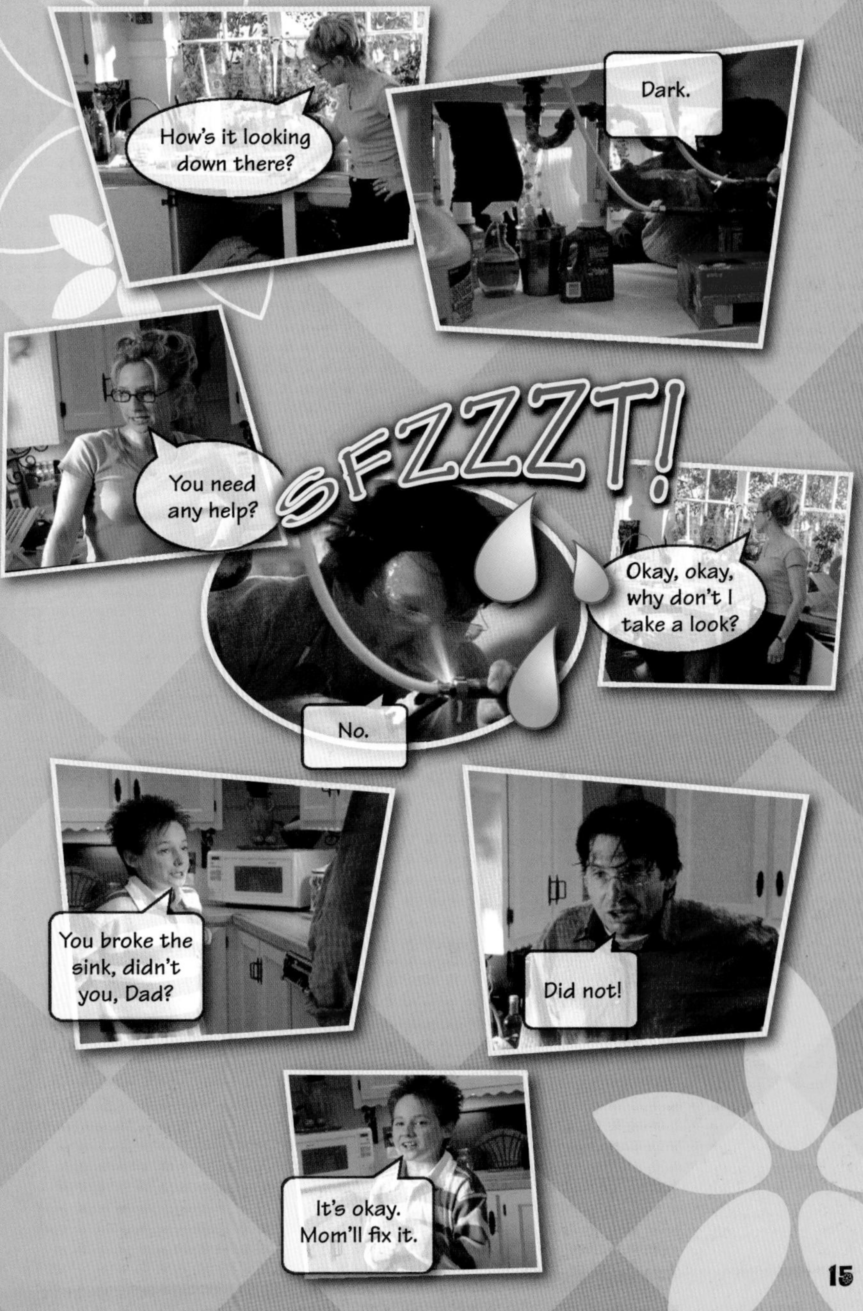
How's it looking down there?
Dark.
You need any help?
SFZZZT!
Okay, okay, why don't I take a look?
No.
You broke the sink, didn't you, Dad?
Did not!
It's okay. Mom'll fix it.

Mom, Mom, she's our man, if she can't fix it, no one can! Goooo Mom!"
Hey, what about me? I tried. Where's my cheer?
Don't worry, Dad, I'll come up with a cheer for you. I need all the practice I can get.
Why?
Lanny and I are trying out for cheerleading tomorrow.
Cheerleading?
"Dad, Dad, he's our man, if he can't fix it, Mom sure can! Goooo Mom!"

AT HOME...

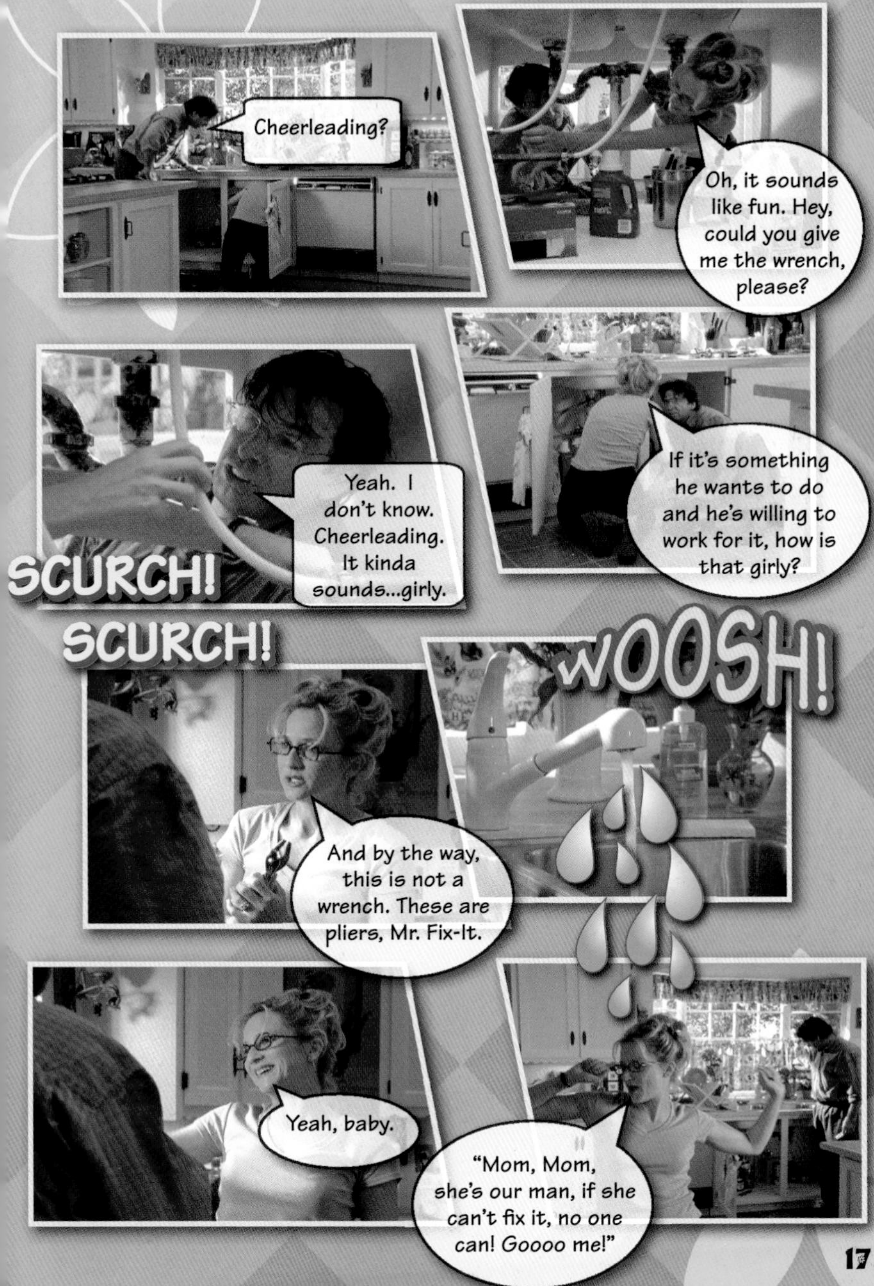

Cheerleading?
Oh, it sounds like fun. Hey, could you give me the wrench, please?
Yeah. I don't know. Cheerleading. It kinda sounds...girly.
SCURCH!
SCURCH!
If it's something he wants to do and he's willing to work for it, how is that girly?
And by the way, this is not a wrench. These are pliers, Mr. Fix-It.
WOOSH!
Yeah, baby.
"Mom, Mom, she's our man, if she can't fix it, no one can! Goooo me!"

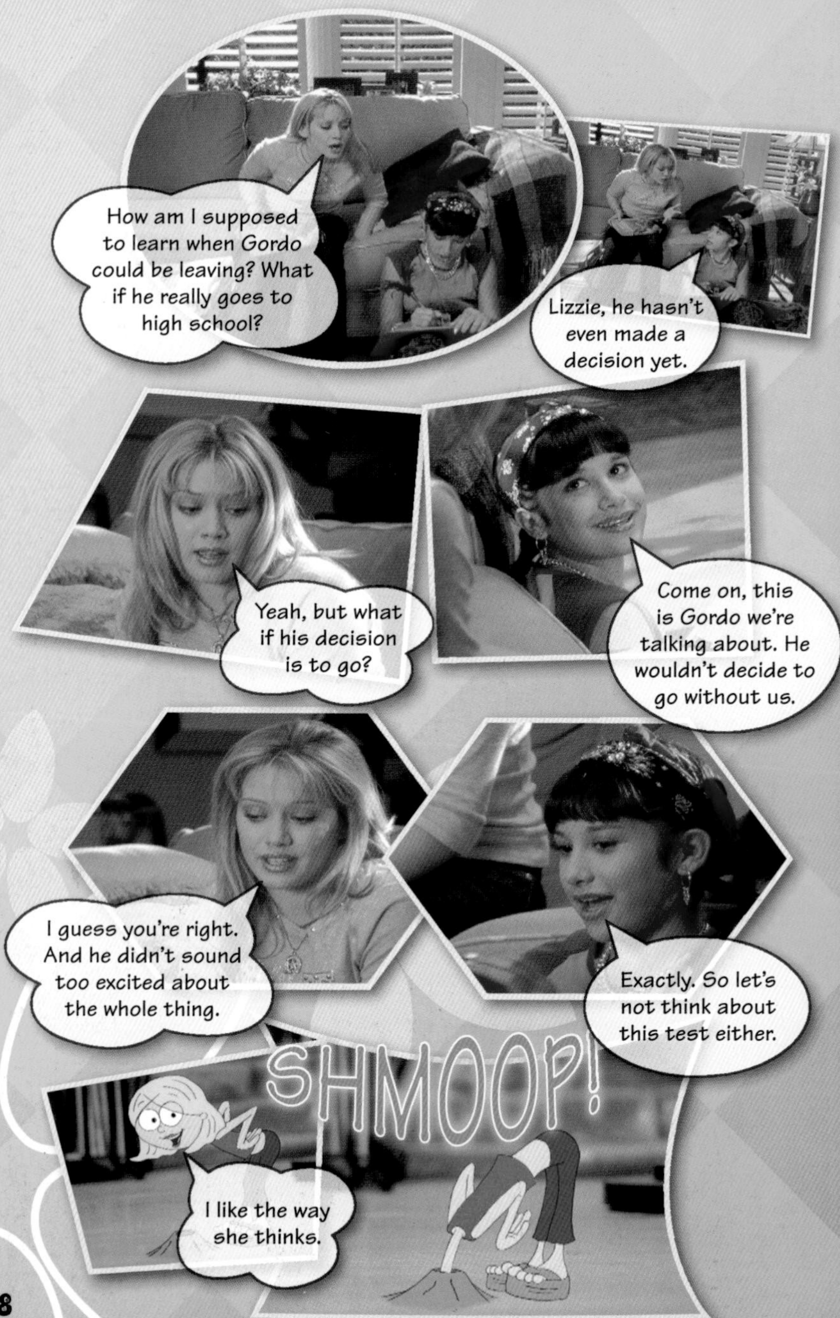
How am I supposed to learn when Gordo could be leaving? What if he really goes to high school?
Lizzie, he hasn't even made a decision yet.
Yeah, but what if his decision is to go?
Come on, this is Gordo we're talking about. He wouldn't decide to go without us.
I guess you're right. And he didn't sound too excited about the whole thing.
Exactly. So let's not think about this test either.
SHMOOP!
I like the way she thinks.

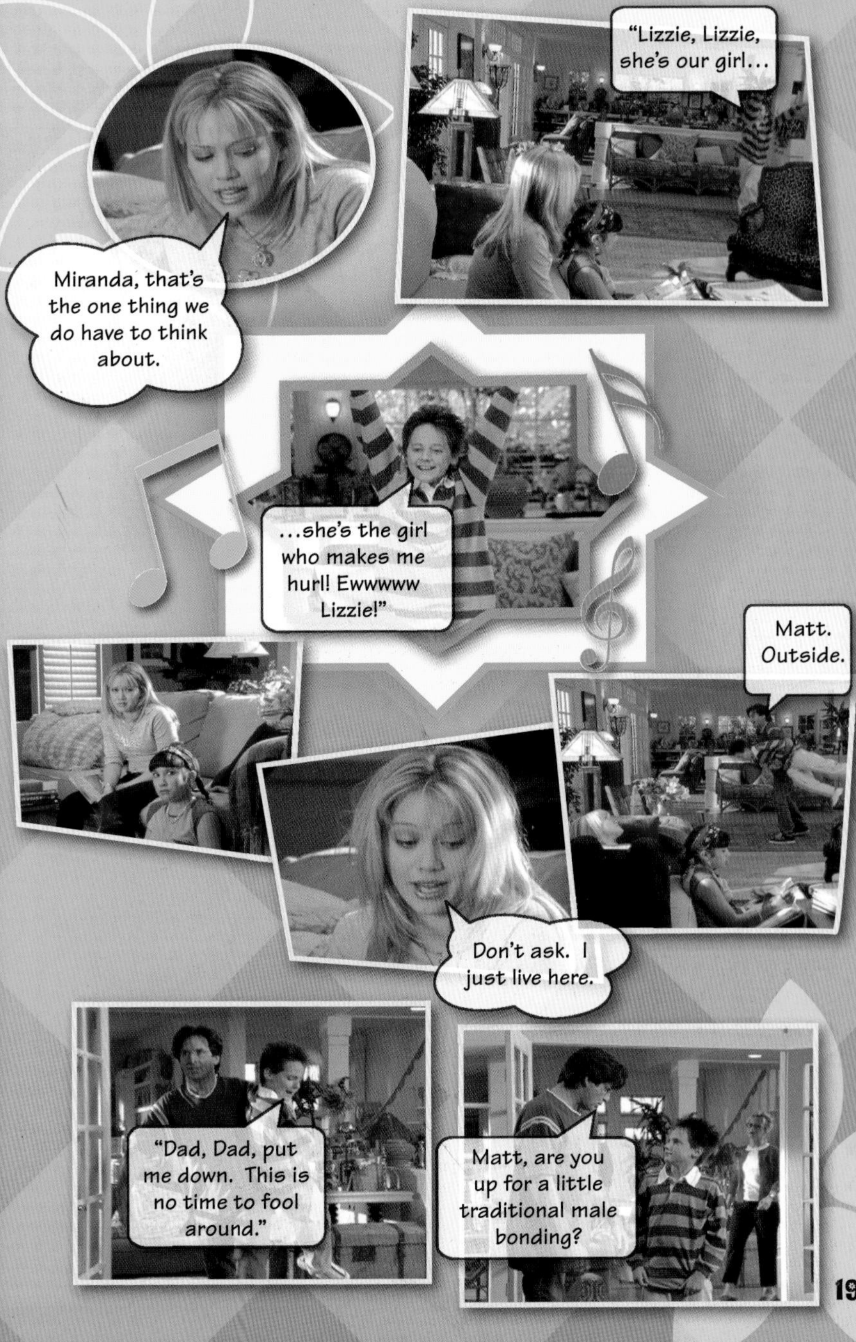
Miranda, that's the one thing we do have to think about.
"Lizzie, Lizzie, she's our girl...
...she's the girl who makes me hurl! Ewwwww Lizzie!"
Matt. Outside.
Don't ask. I just live here.
"Dad, Dad, put me down. This is no time to fool around."
Matt, are you up for a little traditional male bonding?

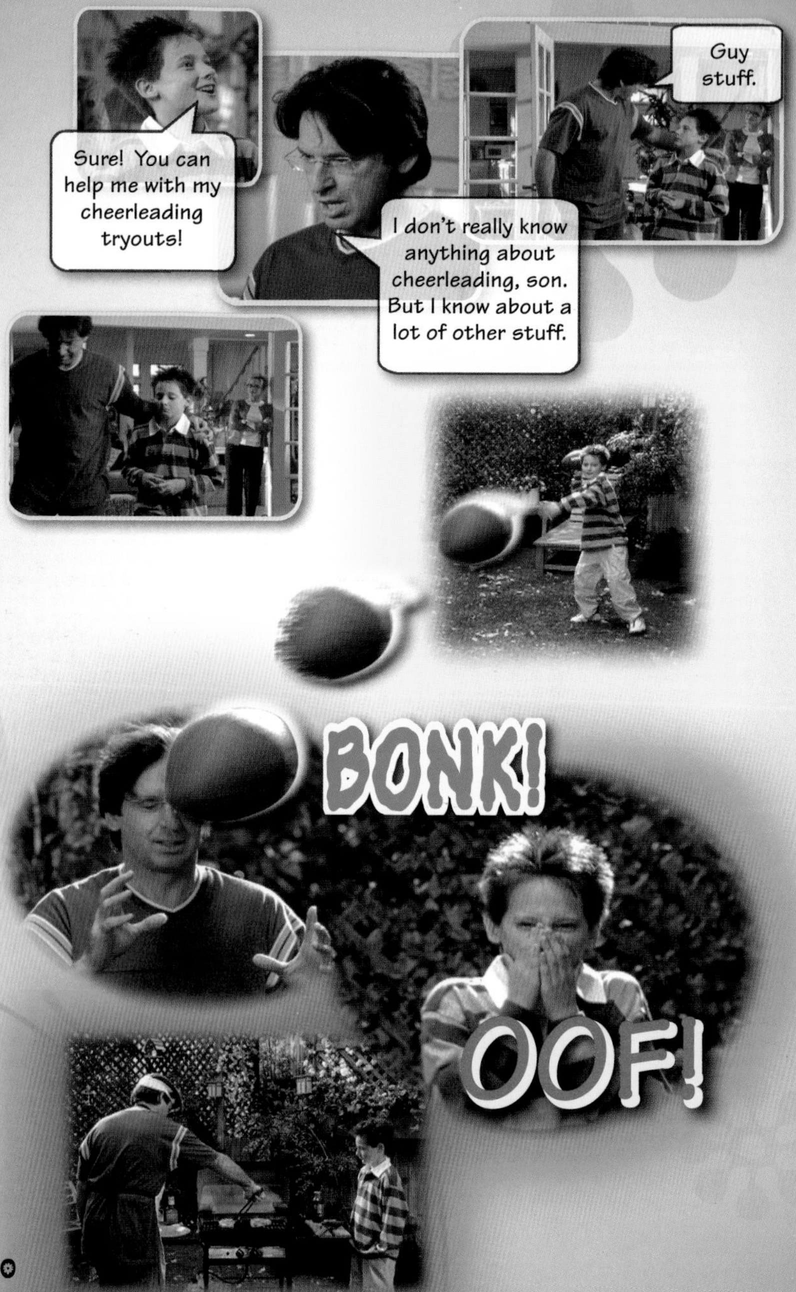
Sure! You can help me with my cheerleading tryouts!
I don't really know anything about cheerleading, son. But I know about a lot of other stuff.
Guy stuff.
BONK!
OOF!

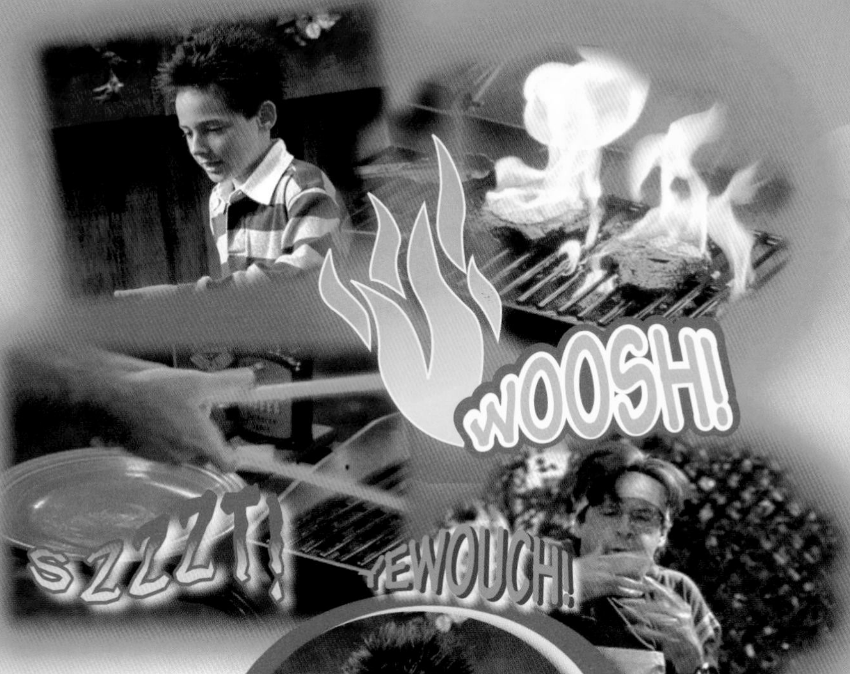
WOOSH!
SZZZT!
YEWOUCH!
OH NO!

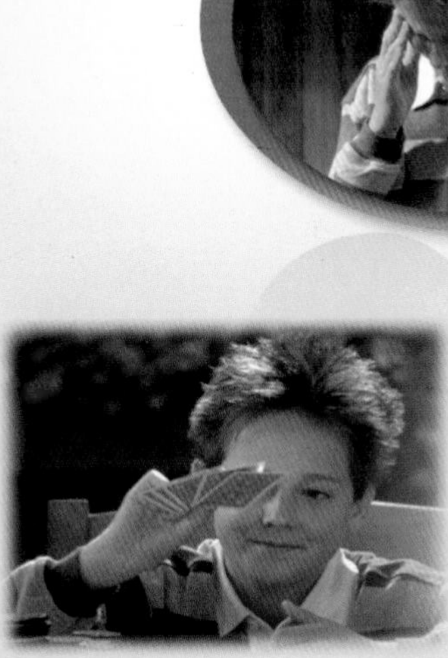

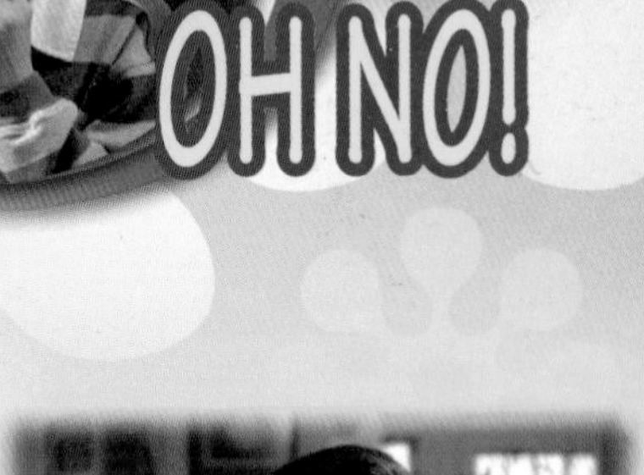

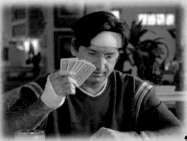

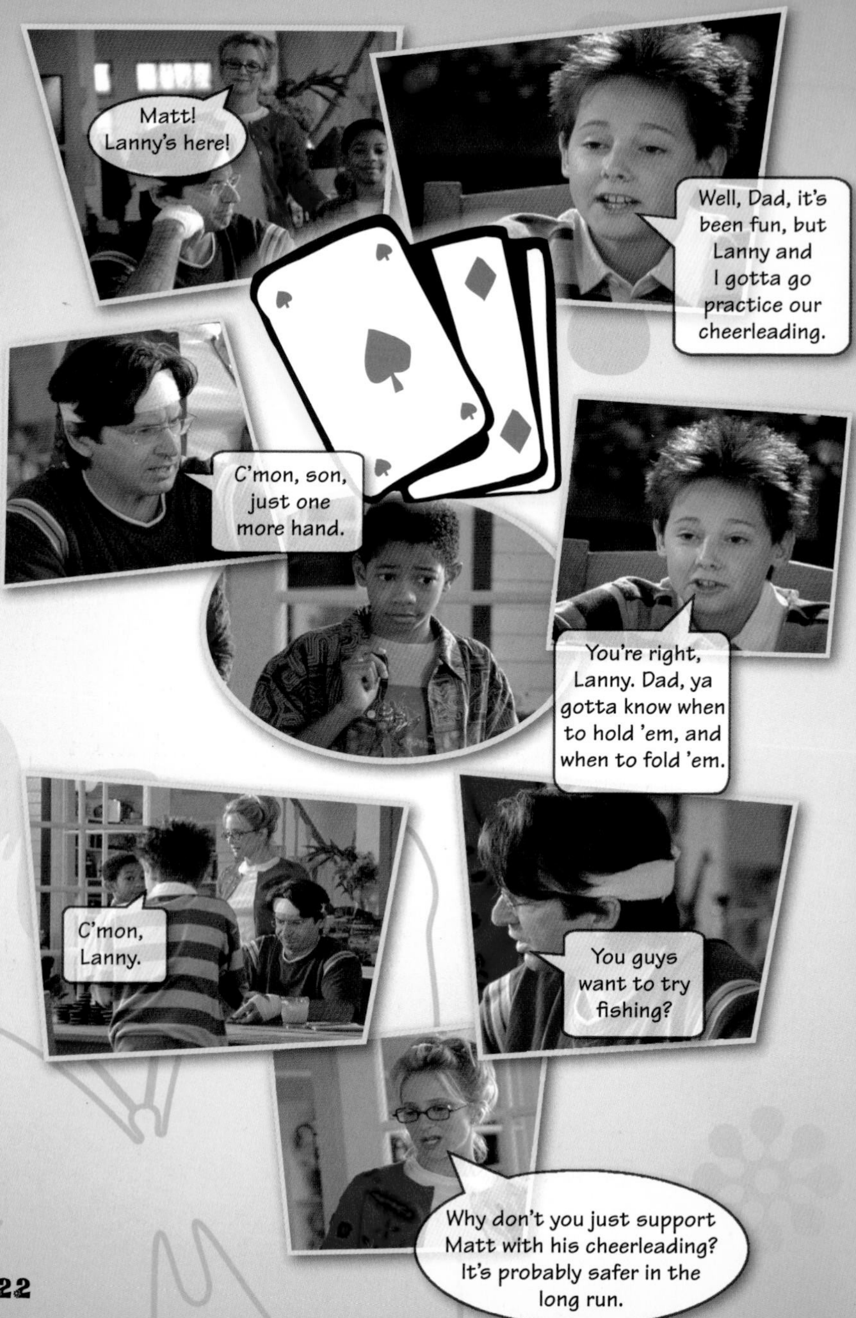
Matt! Lanny's here!
Well, Dad, it's been fun, but Lanny and I gotta go practice our cheerleading.
C'mon, son, just one more hand.
You're right, Lanny. Dad, ya gotta know when to hold 'em, and when to fold 'em.
C'mon, Lanny.
You guys want to try fishing?
Why don't you just support Matt with his cheerleading? It's probably safer in the long run.

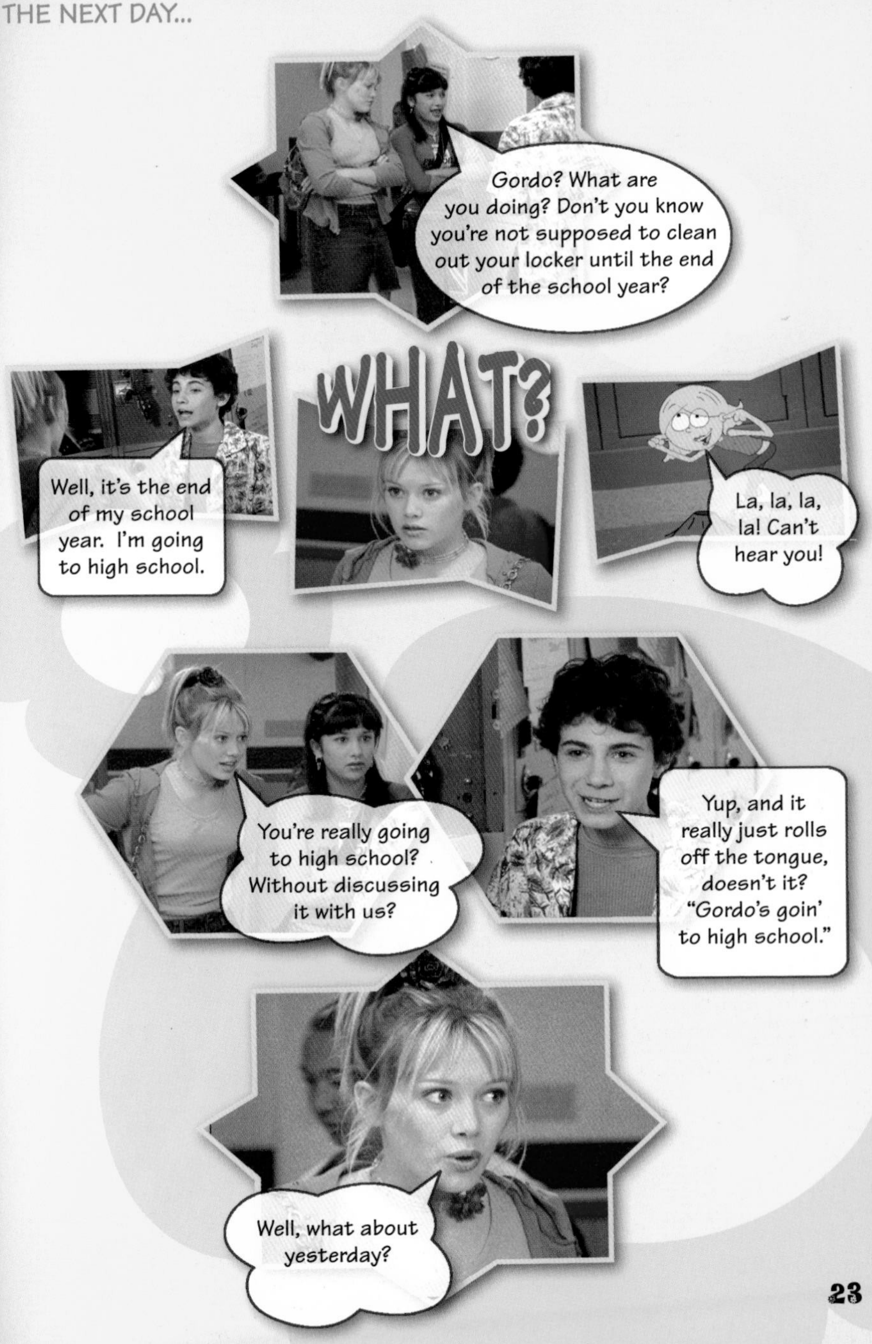
THE NEXT DAY...
Gordo? What are you doing? Don't you know you're not supposed to clean out your locker until the end of the school year?
Well, it's the end of my school year. I'm going to high school.
WHAT?
La, la, la, la! Can't hear you!
You're really going to high school? Without discussing it with us?
Yup, and it really just rolls off the tongue, doesn't it? "Gordo's goin' to high school."
Well, what about yesterday?

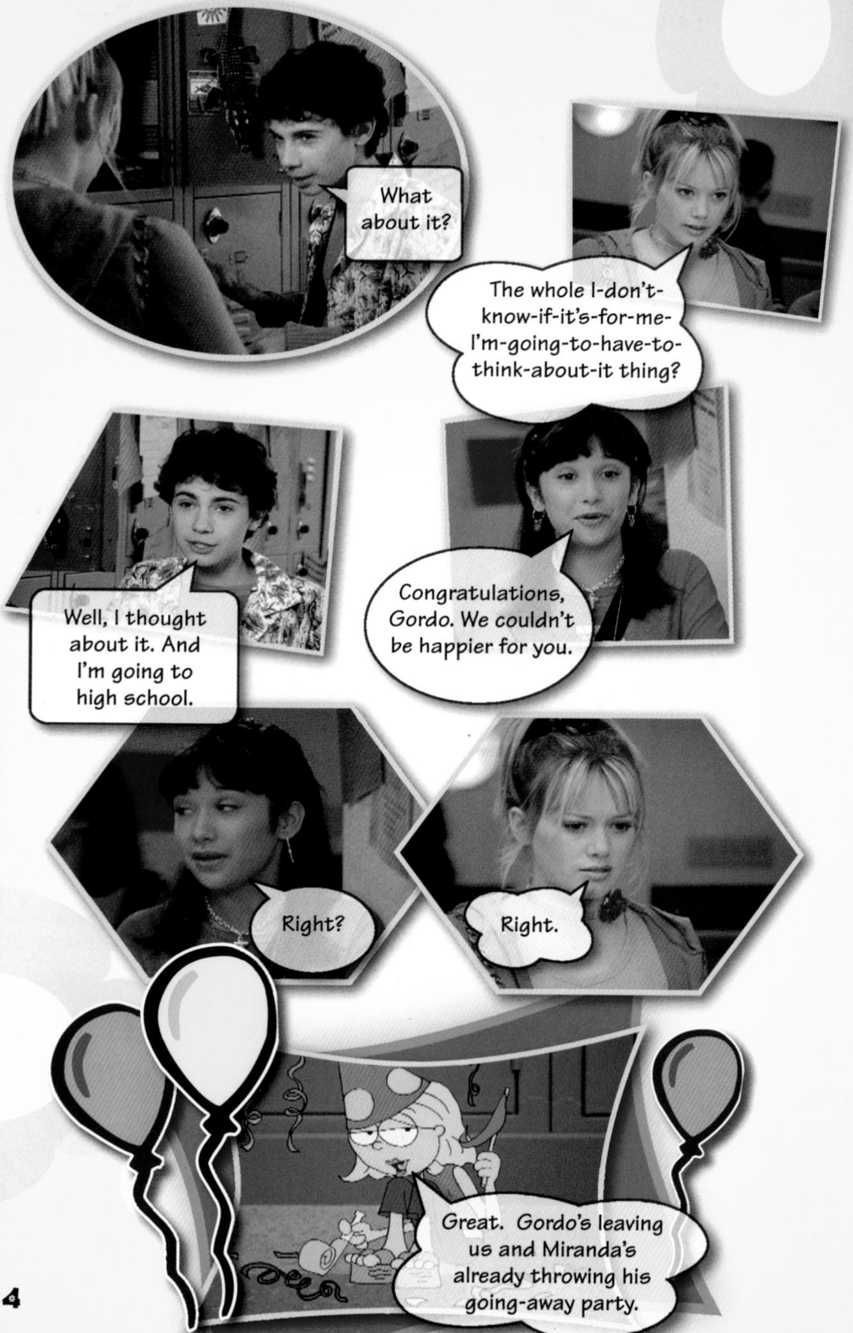
What about it?
The whole I-don't-know-if-it's-for-me-I'm-going-to-have-to-think-about-it thing?
Well, I thought about it. And I'm going to high school.
Congratulations, Gordo. We couldn't be happier for you.
Right?
Right.
Great. Gordo's leaving us and Miranda's already throwing his going-away party.

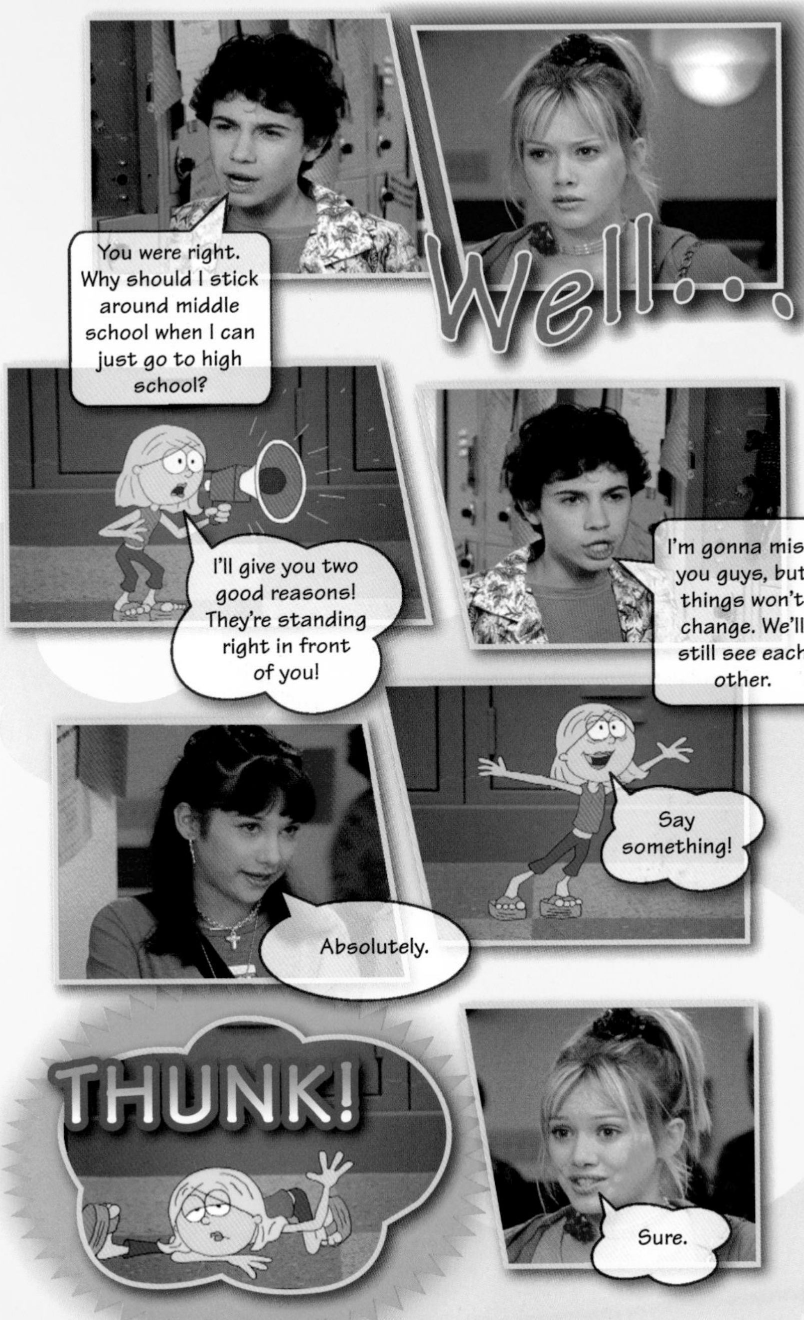

You were right. Why should I stick around middle school when I can just go to high school?
Well...
I'll give you two good reasons! They're standing right in front of you!
I'm gonna miss you guys, but things won't change. We'll still see each other.
Say something!
Absolutely.
THUNK!
Sure.

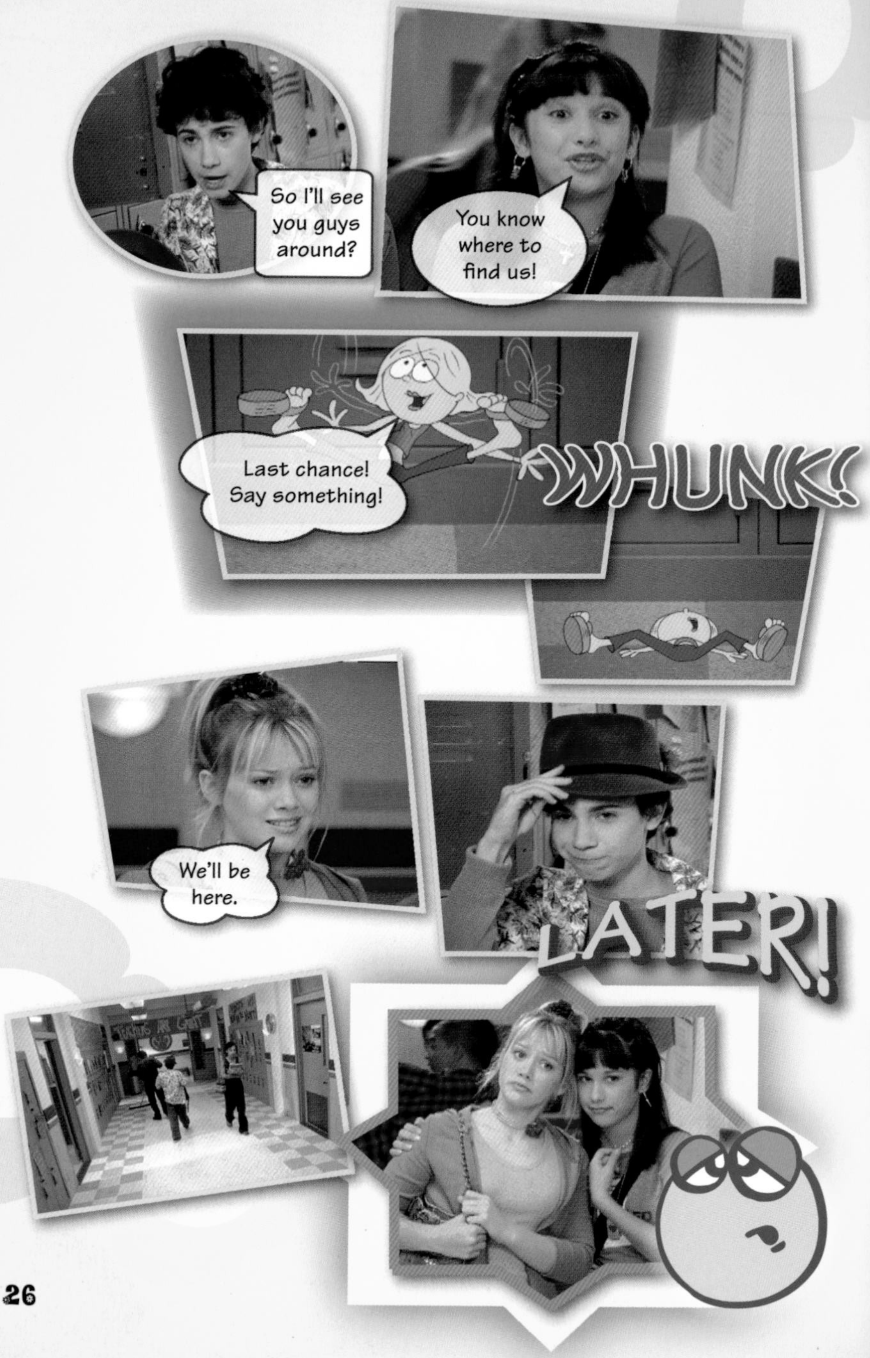
So I'll see you guys around?
You know where to find us!
Last chance! Say something!
WHUNK!
We'll be here.
LATER!

HIGH SCHOOL...

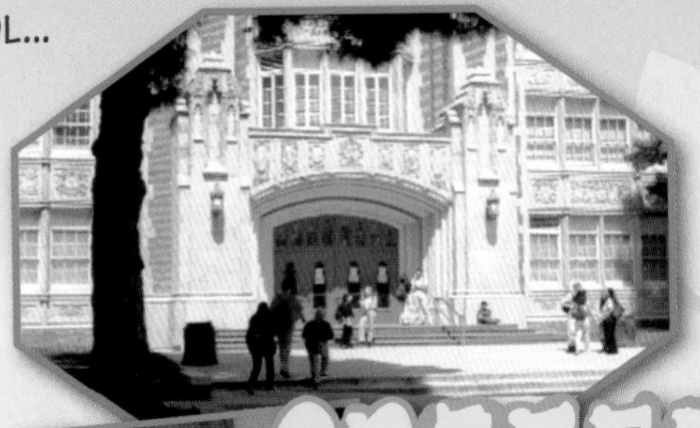

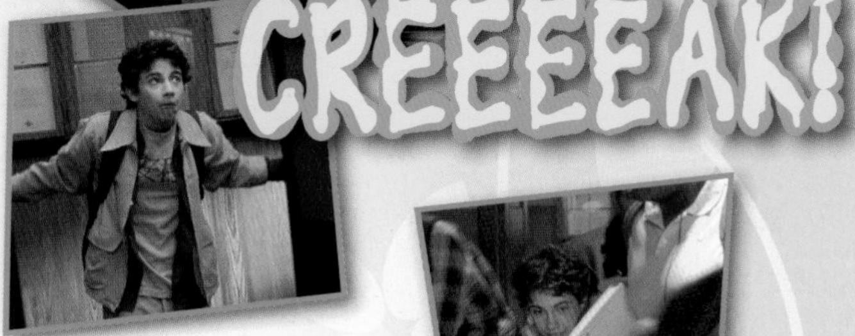
CREEEEAK!

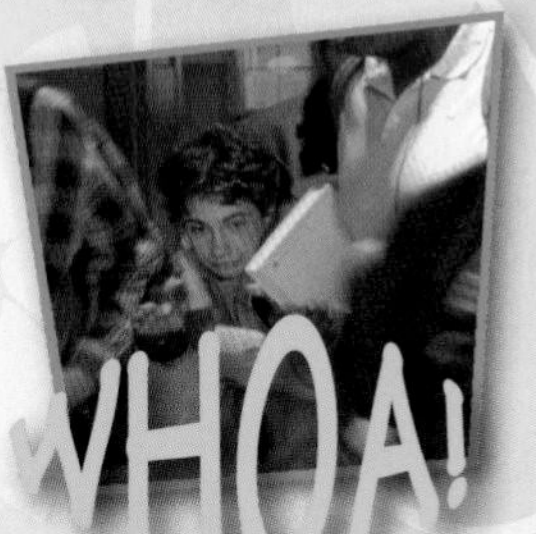
WHOA!

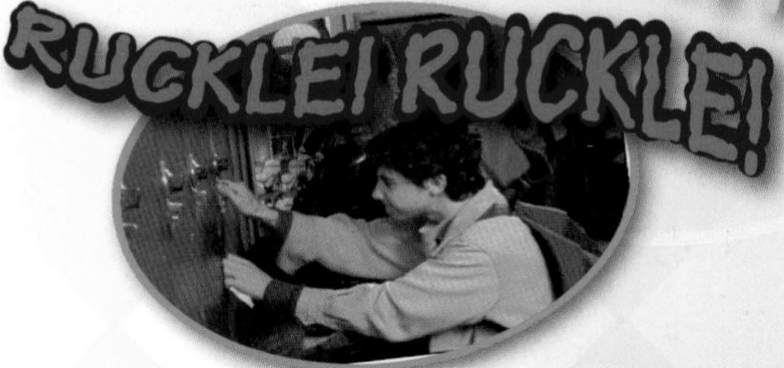
RUCKLE! RUCKLE!

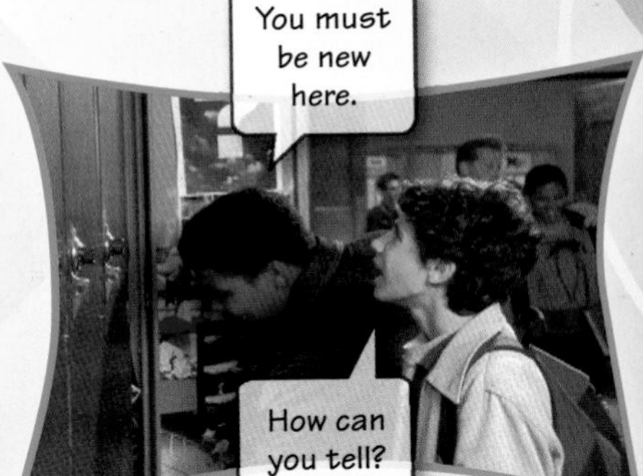
You must be new here.
How can you tell?

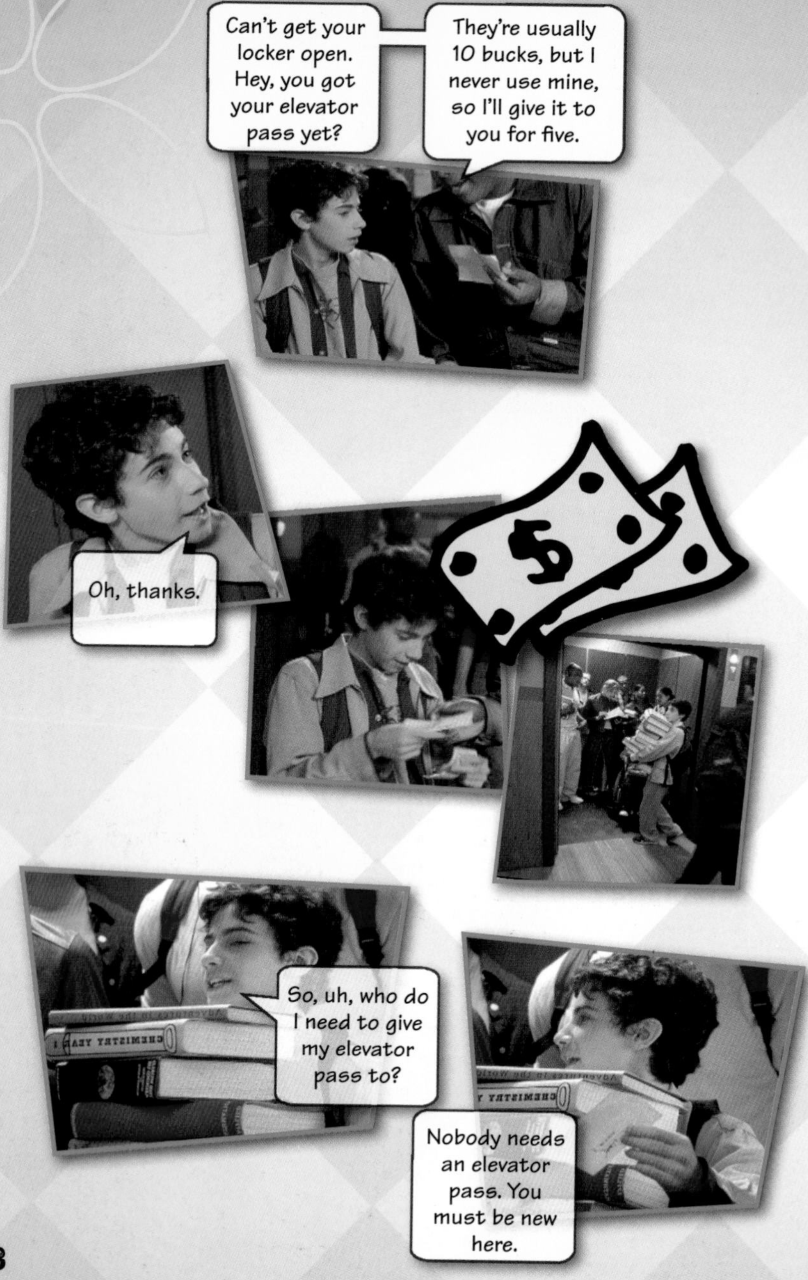

Can't get your locker open. Hey, you got your elevator pass yet?
They're usually 10 bucks, but I never use mine, so I'll give it to you for five.
Oh, thanks.
So, uh, who do I need to give my elevator pass to?
Nobody needs an elevator pass. You must be new here.

AT LUNCH...

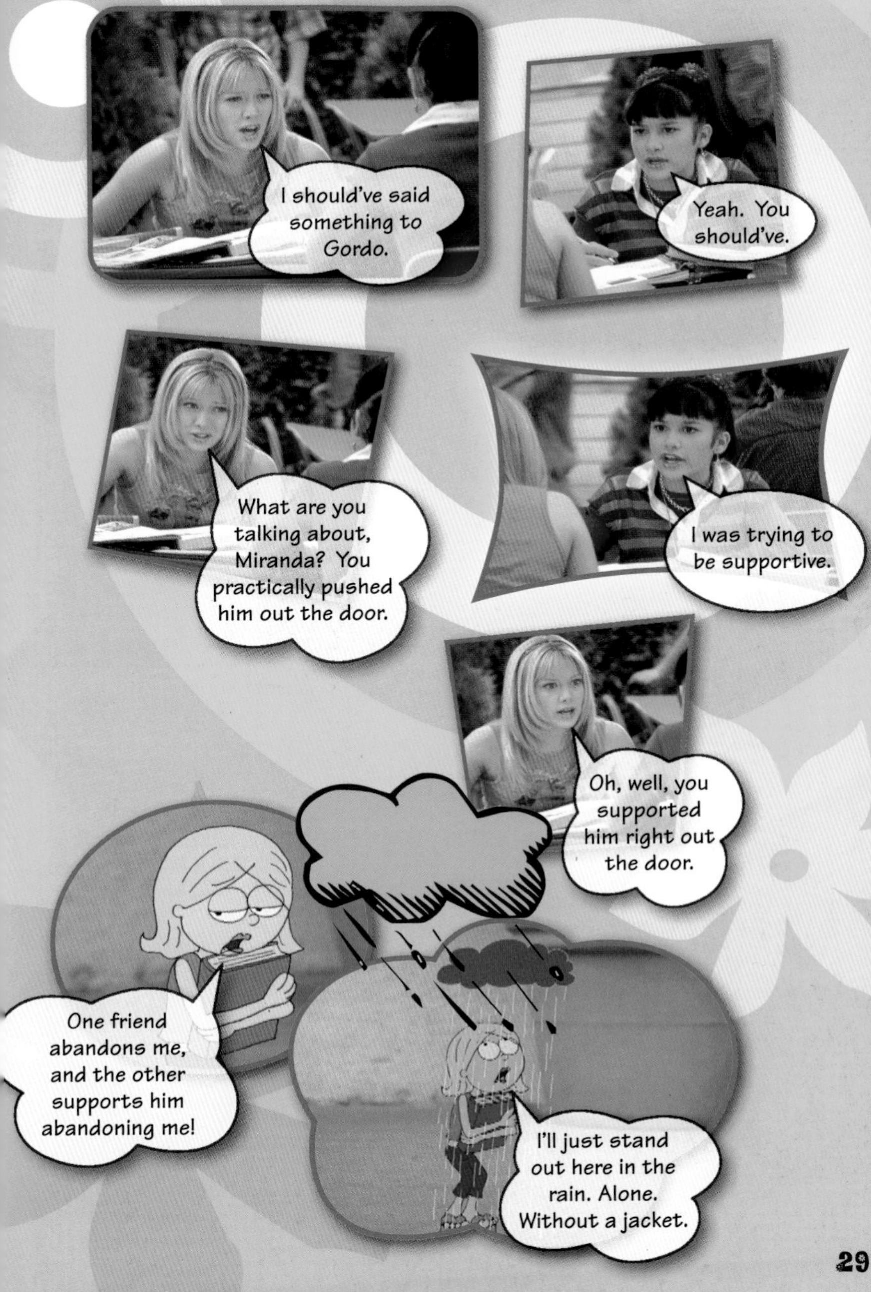
I should've said something to Gordo.
Yeah. You should've.
What are you talking about, Miranda? You practically pushed him out the door.
I was trying to be supportive.
Oh, well, you supported him right out the door.
One friend abandons me, and the other supports him abandoning me!
I'll just stand out here in the rain. Alone. Without a jacket.

Lizzie, I'm sorry. But what can we do? He's gone.
I just didn't actually think he'd leave.
Me neither. But this is a huge deal for Gordo.
Well, it's a huge deal for us, too.
Lizzie, he's not doing this to us, he's doing it for him. C'mon! Friends should always want the best for each other.
Yeah, but what about me?
I know you're right. But I guess I just should've said something.

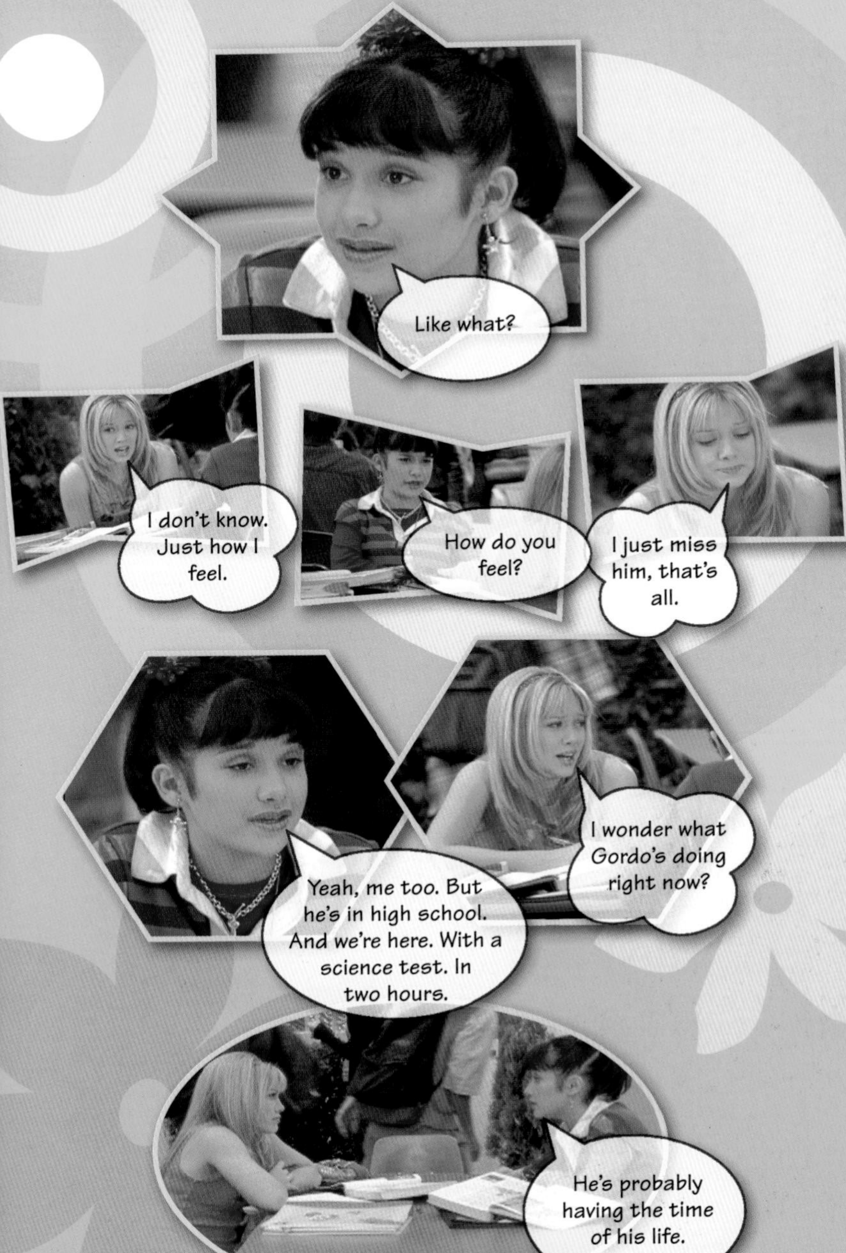
Like what?
I don't know. Just how I feel.
How do you feel?
I just miss him, that's all.
I wonder what Gordo's doing right now?
Yeah, me too. But he's in high school. And we're here. With a science test. In two hours.
He's probably having the time of his life.

BACK AT HIGH SCHOOL...

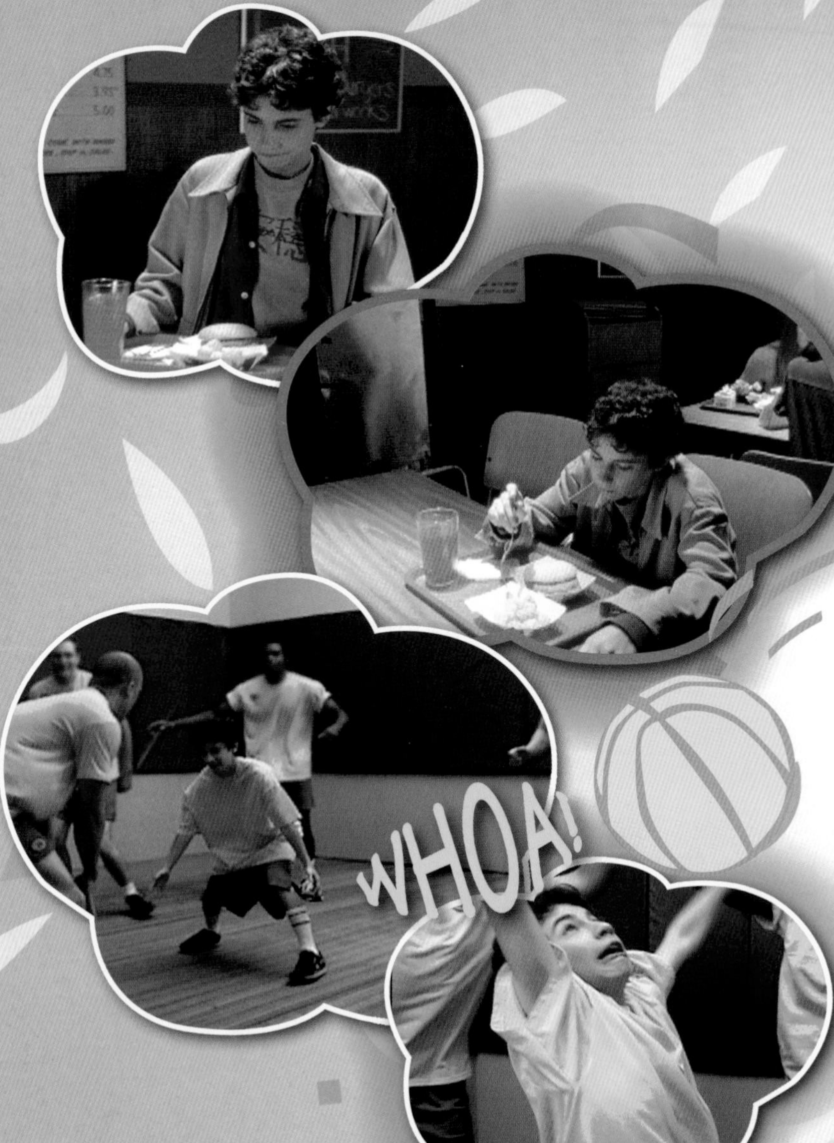
WHOA!

LATER THAT AFTERNOON...

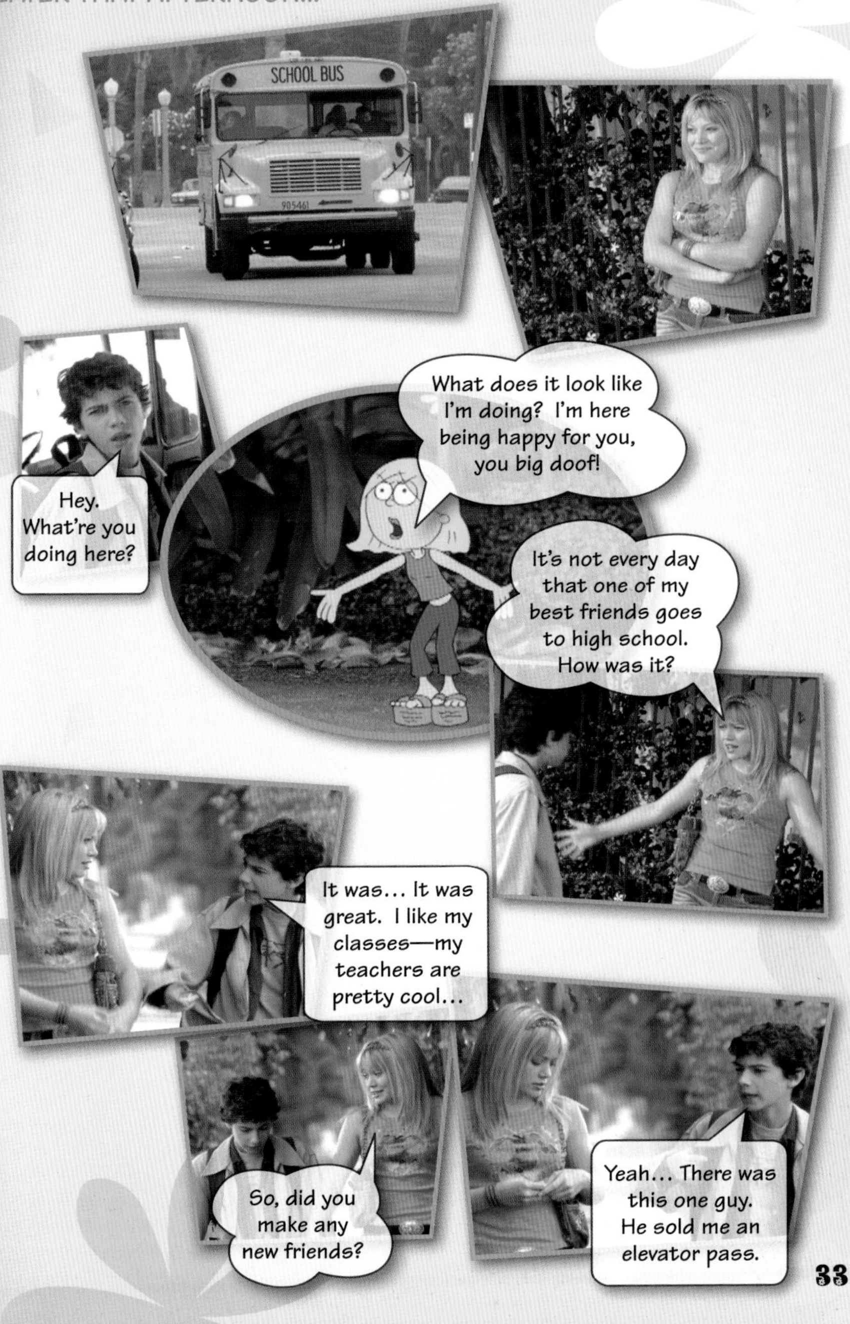

SCHOOL BUS
Hey. What're you doing here?
What does it look like I'm doing? I'm here being happy for you, you big doof!
It's not every day that one of my best friends goes to high school. How was it?
It was... It was great. I like my classes—my teachers are pretty cool...
So, did you make any new friends?
Yeah... There was this one guy. He sold me an elevator pass.

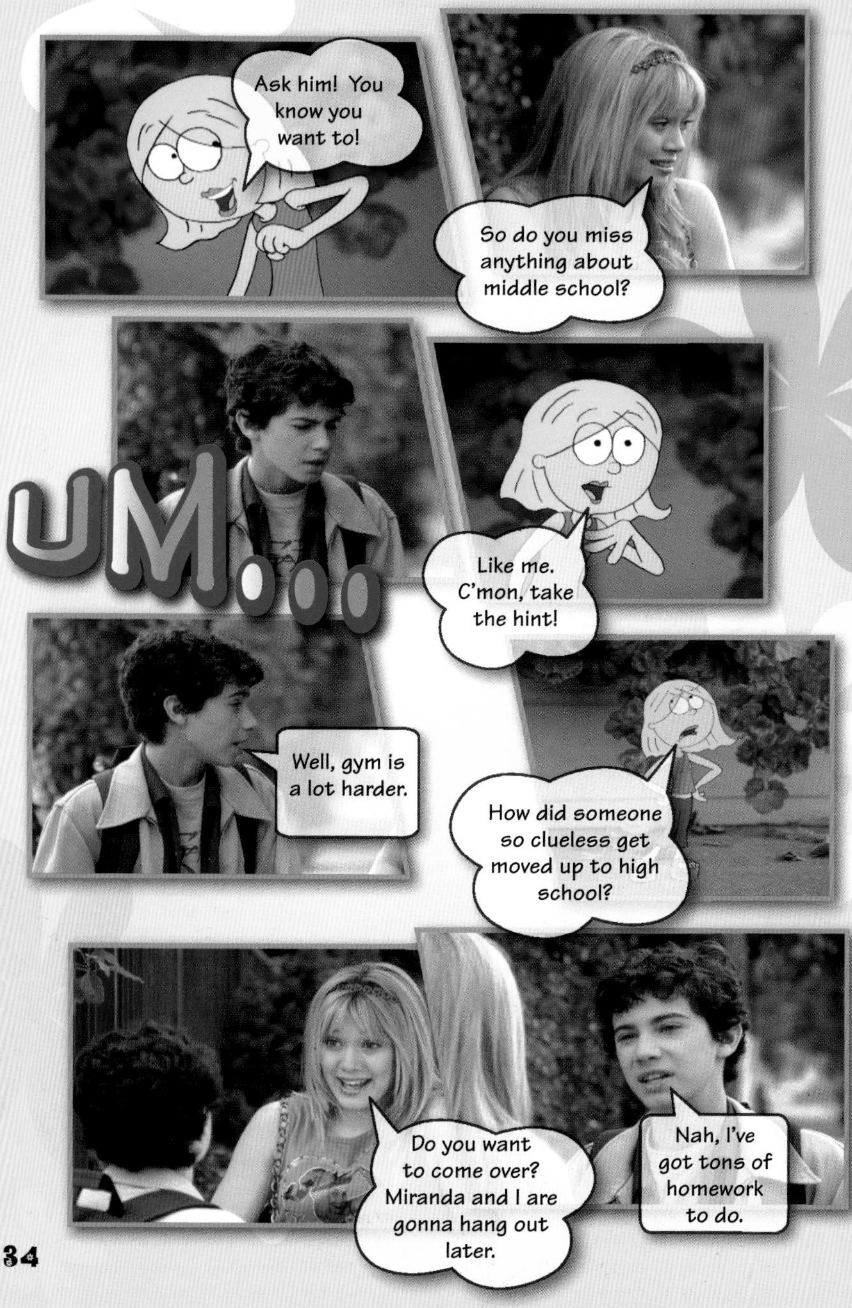

Ask him! You know you want to!
So do you miss anything about middle school?
UM...
Like me. C'mon, take the hint!
Well, gym is a lot harder.
How did someone so clueless get moved up to high school?
Do you want to come over? Miranda and I are gonna hang out later.
Nah, I've got tons of homework to do.

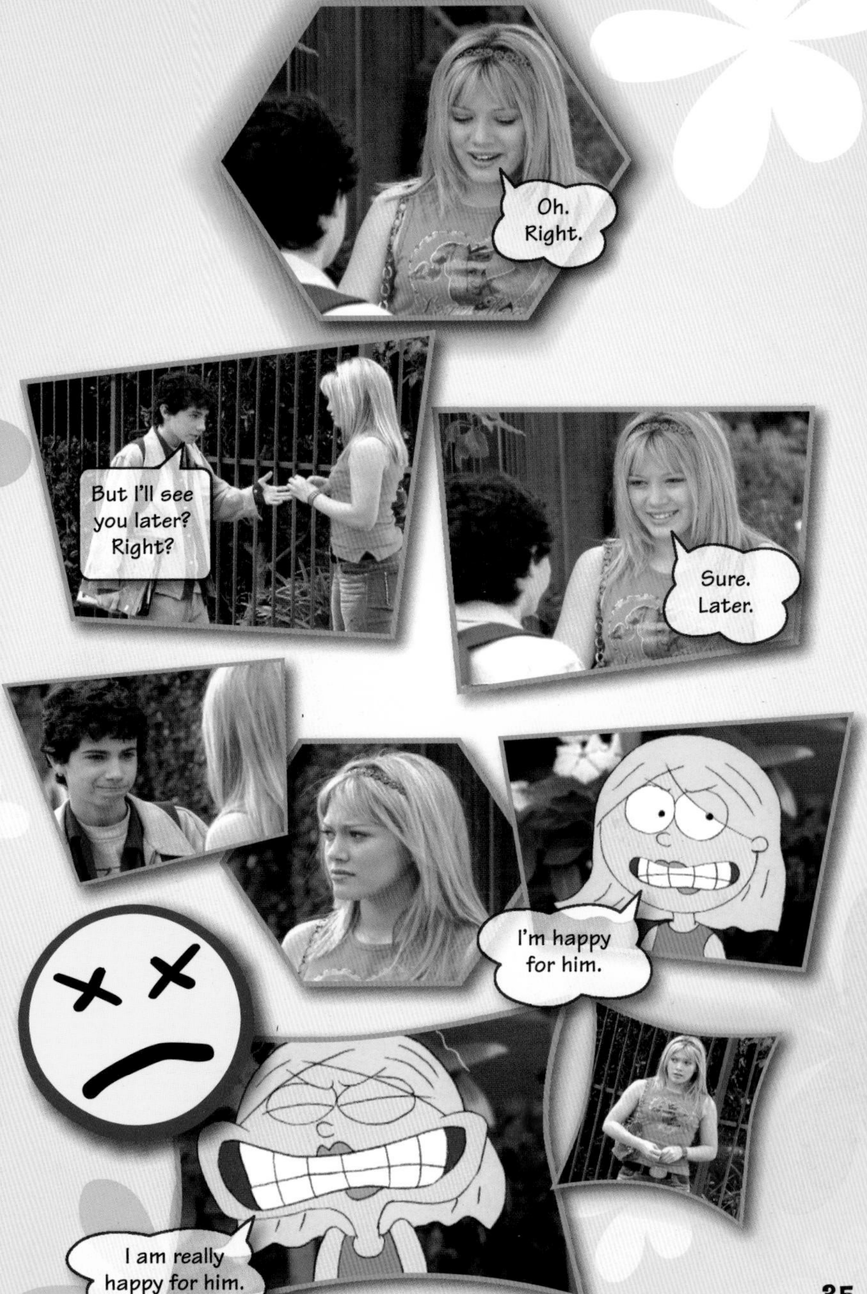
Oh. Right.
But I'll see you later? Right?
Sure. Later.
I'm happy for him.
I am really happy for him.

AT HOME...

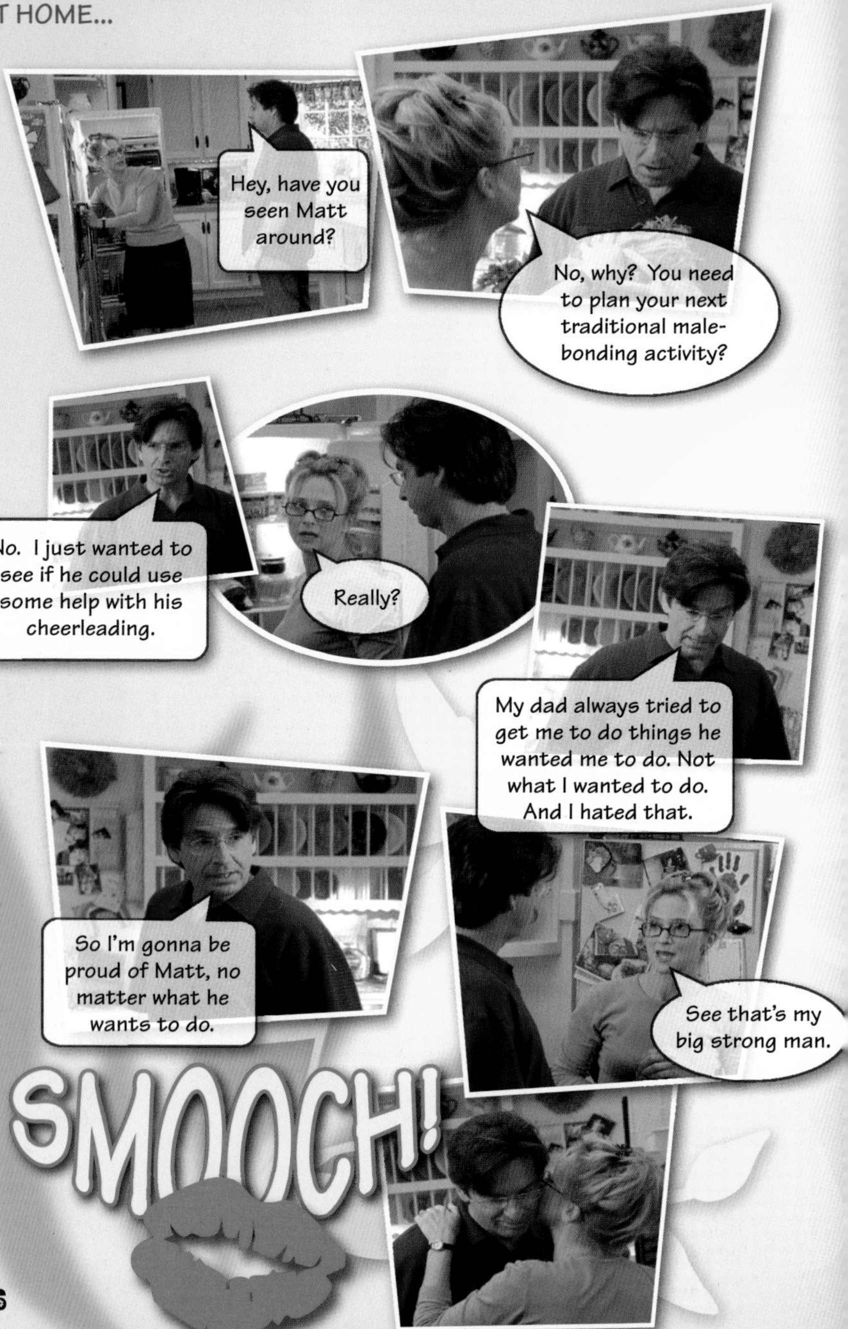

Hey, have you seen Matt around?
No, why? You need to plan your next traditional male-bonding activity?
No. I just wanted to see if he could use some help with his cheerleading.
Really?
My dad always tried to get me to do things he wanted me to do. Not what I wanted to do. And I hated that.
So I'm gonna be proud of Matt, no matter what he wants to do.
See that's my big strong man.
SMOOCH!

MEANWHIILE AT CHEERLEADING TRYOUTS...
I'd like to welcome everyone to cheerleading tryouts! I wish we could take all of you...
...but we can't. We're looking for five new girls and only one new boy.
So let's stop being students and start being cheerleaders! Matt McGuire, you're up!
One person at a time!
CLICK!
I said one person at a time!
YEAH!

wOOSH!
WOO-HOO!
YEAH!
YEAH!
That was the greatest routine I have ever seen. So which one of you wants to be a cheerleader?
But...but we were both great! And we worked so hard!
We only have one boy's uniform.
Keep your uniform. No one splits up Matt and Lanny.

AT HOME...

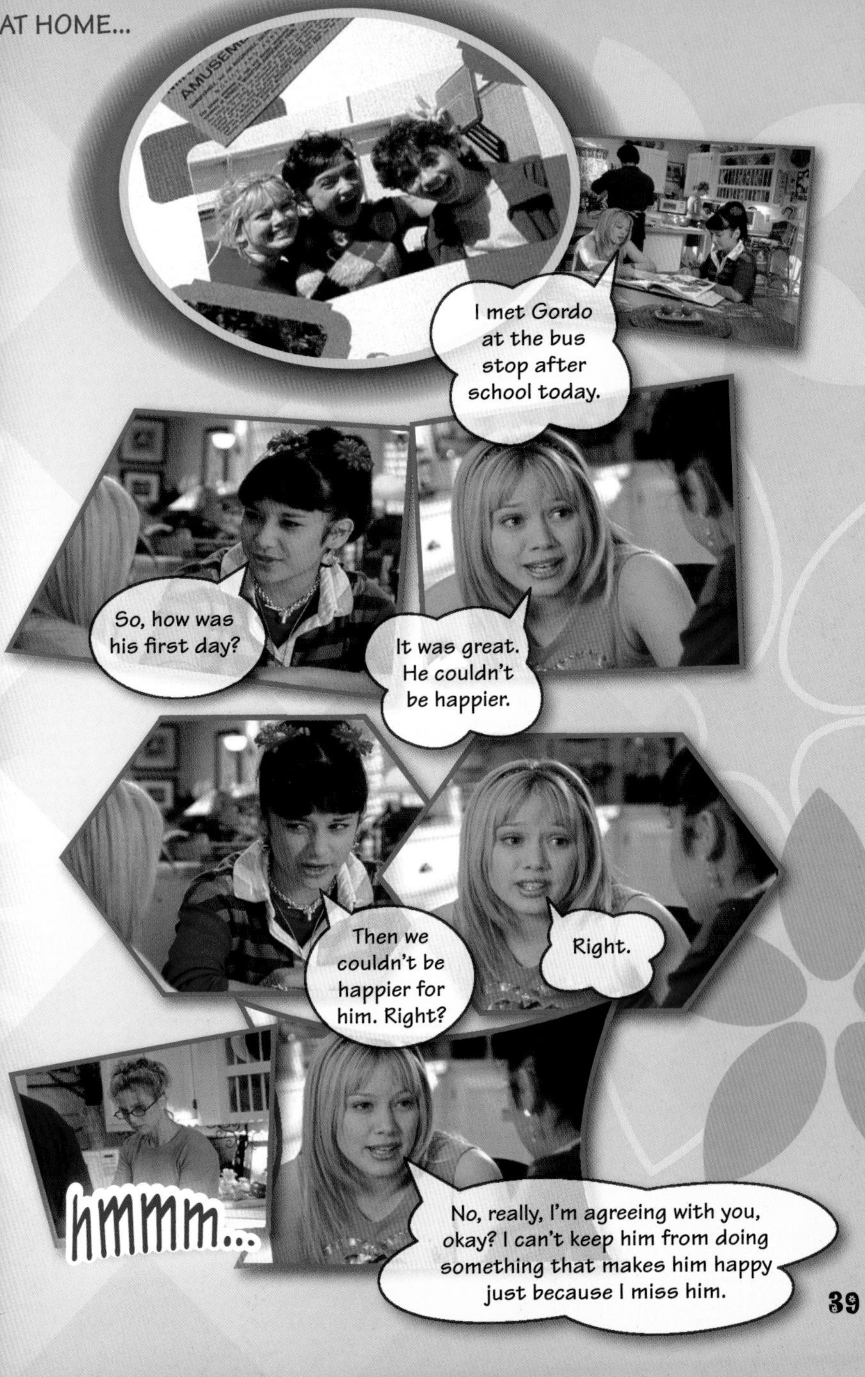
AMUSEM
I met Gordo at the bus stop after school today.
So, how was his first day?
It was great. He couldn't be happier.
Then we couldn't be happier for him. Right?
Right.
hmmm...
No, really, I'm agreeing with you, okay? I can't keep him from doing something that makes him happy just because I miss him.

You know what, guys? It's really hard growing up.
I mean, you guys have been friends with Gordo for a long time. And things always change. And that's life.
Leave it to Mom to get all Lifetime movie on us.
I just didn't think things would change so soon, you know?
Just because Gordo's going to a different school doesn't mean we're not gonna be friends anymore.
Yeah, but things will certainly be different.
Yeah, they will.

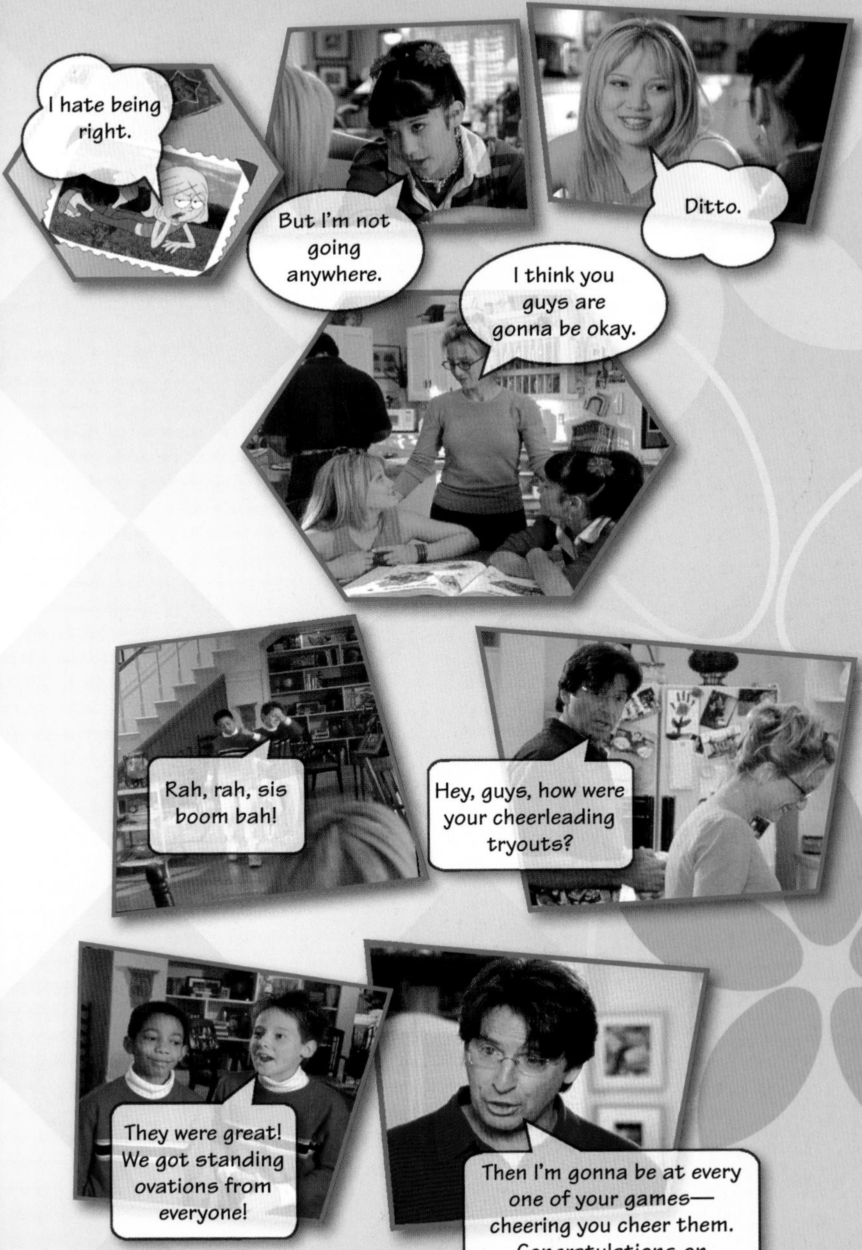
I hate being right.
But I'm not going anywhere.
Ditto.
I think you guys are gonna be okay.
Rah, rah, sis boom bah!
Hey, guys, how were your cheerleading tryouts?
They were great! We got standing ovations from everyone!
Then I'm gonna be at every one of your games—cheering you cheer them. Congratulations on making the team.

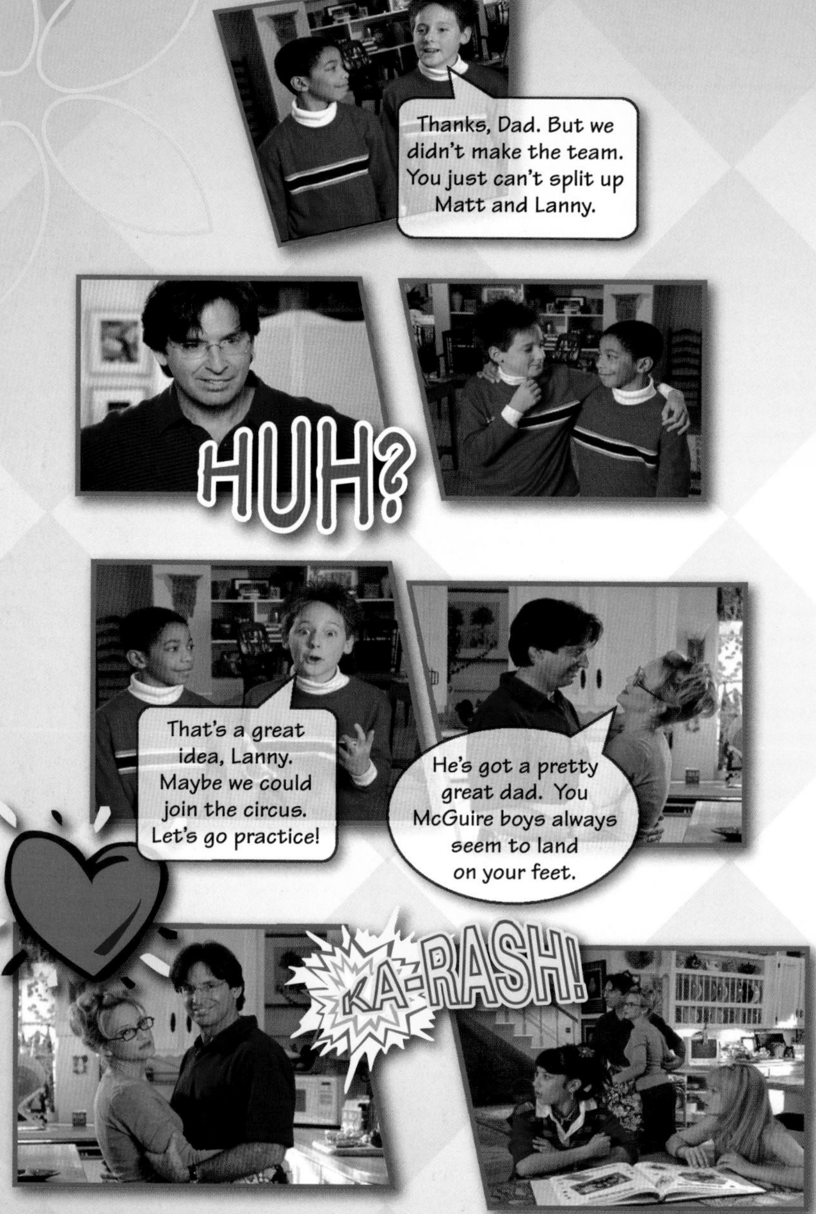

Thanks, Dad. But we didn't make the team. You just can't split up Matt and Lanny.
HUH?
That's a great idea, Lanny. Maybe we could join the circus. Let's go practice!
He's got a pretty great dad. You McGuire boys always seem to land on your feet.
KA-RASH!

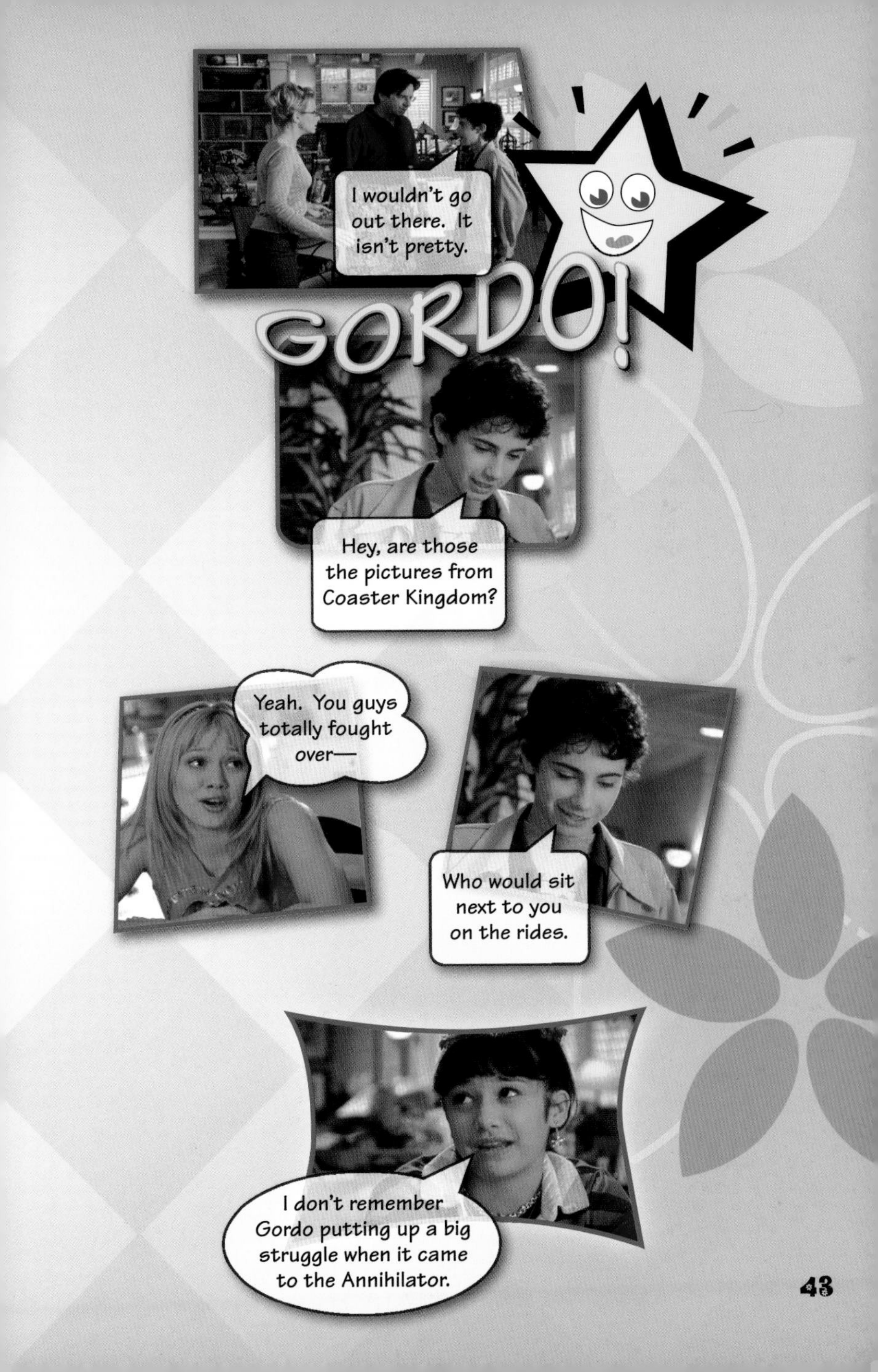
I wouldn't go out there. It isn't pretty.
GORDO!
Hey, are those the pictures from Coaster Kingdom?
Yeah. You guys totally fought over—
Who would sit next to you on the rides.
I don't remember Gordo putting up a big struggle when it came to the Annihilator.

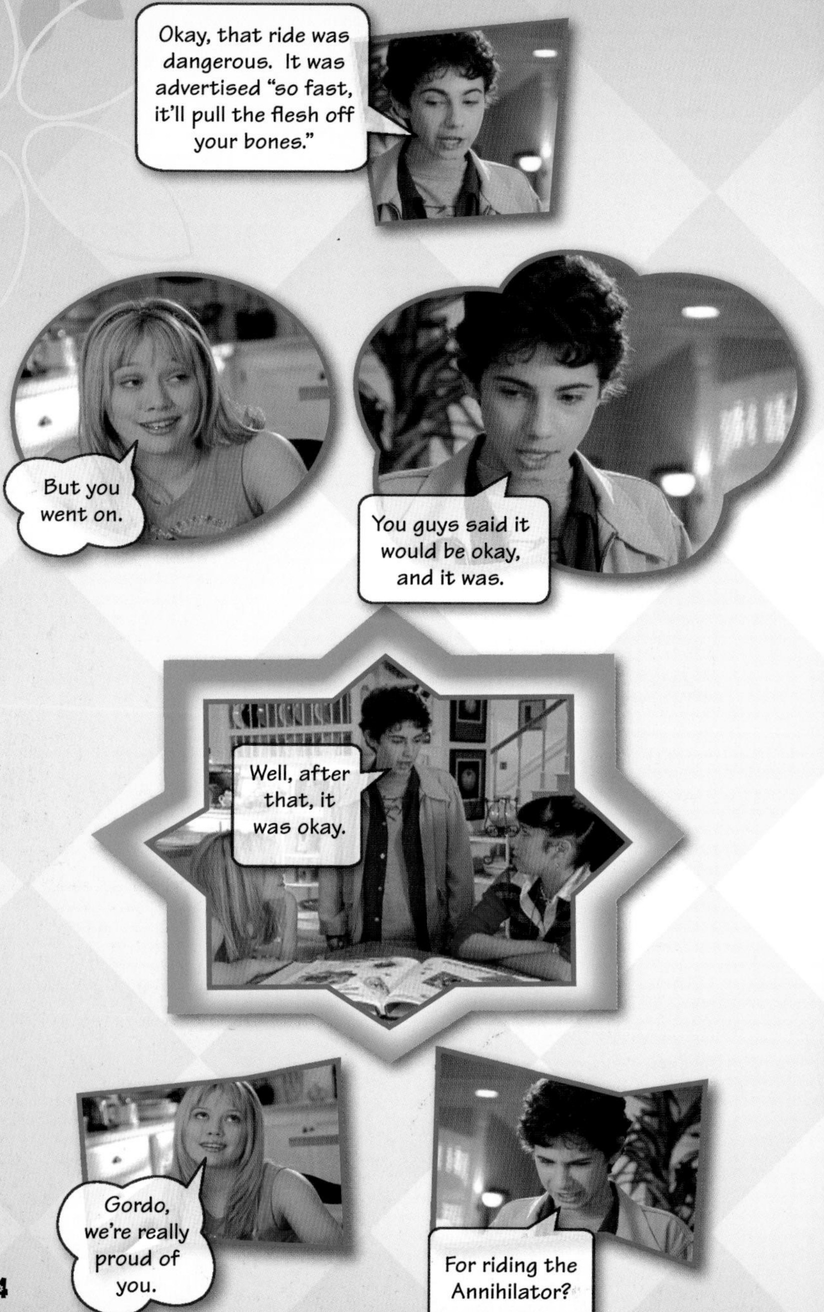

Okay, that ride was dangerous. It was advertised "so fast, it'll pull the flesh off your bones."
But you went on.
You guys said it would be okay, and it was.
Well, after that, it was okay.
Gordo, we're really proud of you.
For riding the Annihilator?

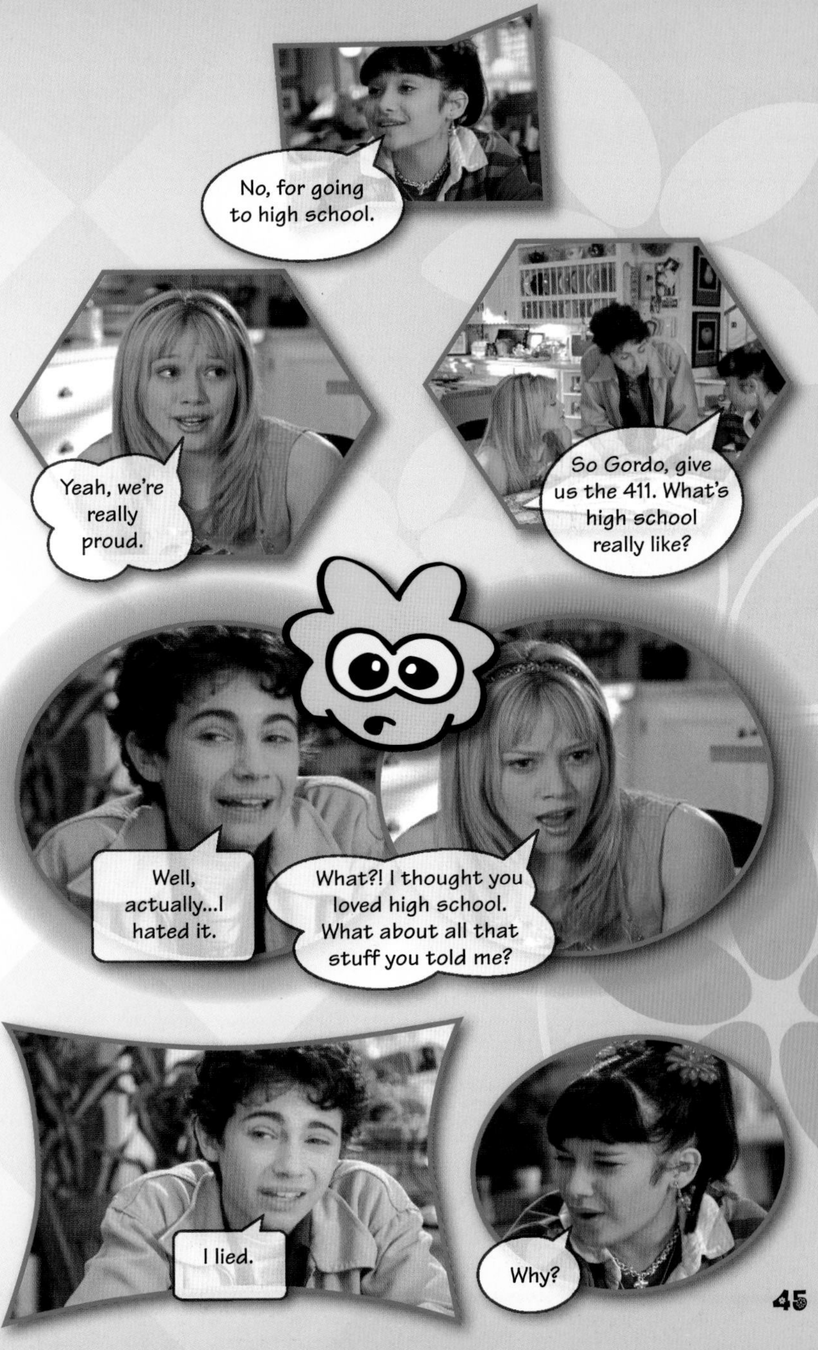
No, for going to high school.
Yeah, we're really proud.
So Gordo, give us the 411. What's high school really like?
Well, actually...I hated it.
What?! I thought you loved high school. What about all that stuff you told me?
I lied.
Why?

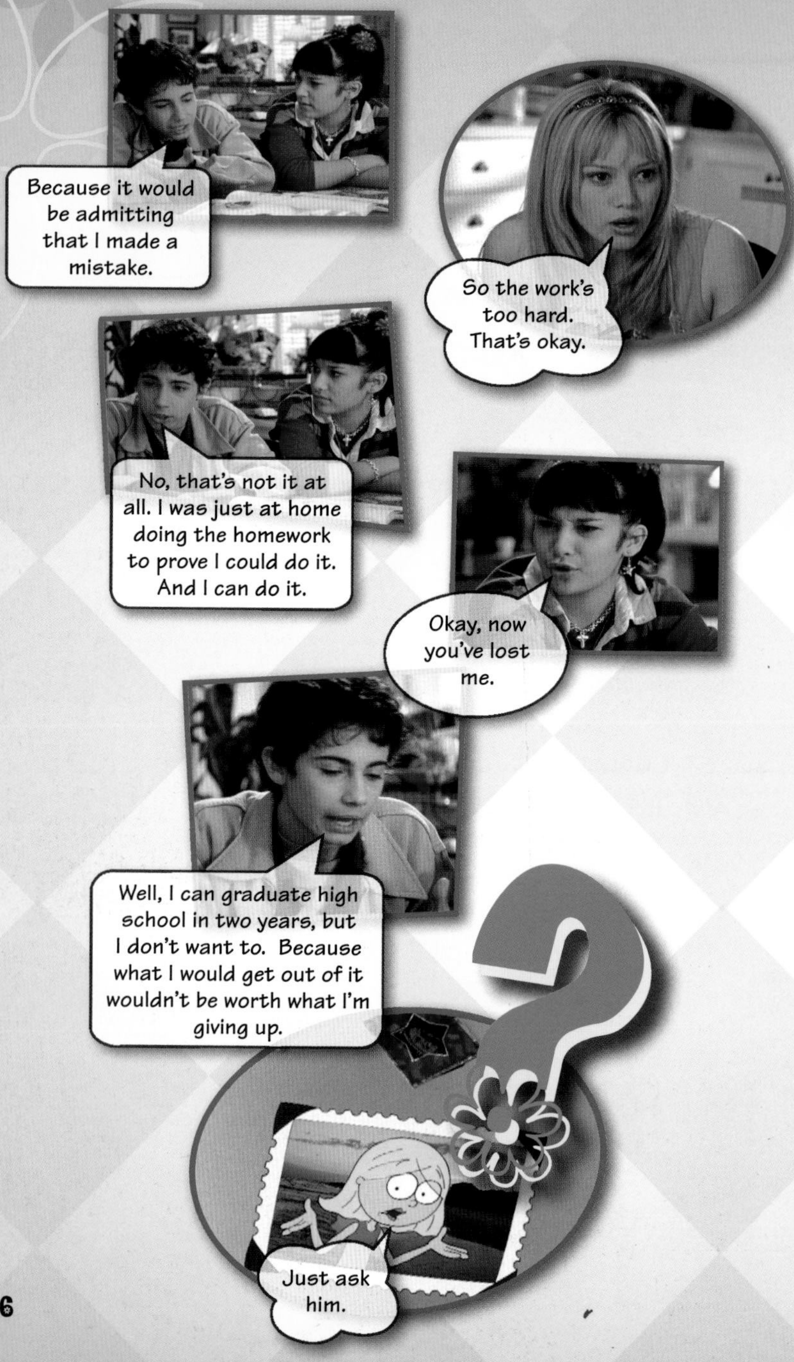
Because it would be admitting that I made a mistake.
So the work's too hard. That's okay.
No, that's not it at all. I was just at home doing the homework to prove I could do it. And I can do it.
Okay, now you've lost me.
Well, I can graduate high school in two years, but I don't want to. Because what I would get out of it wouldn't be worth what I'm giving up.
Just ask him.

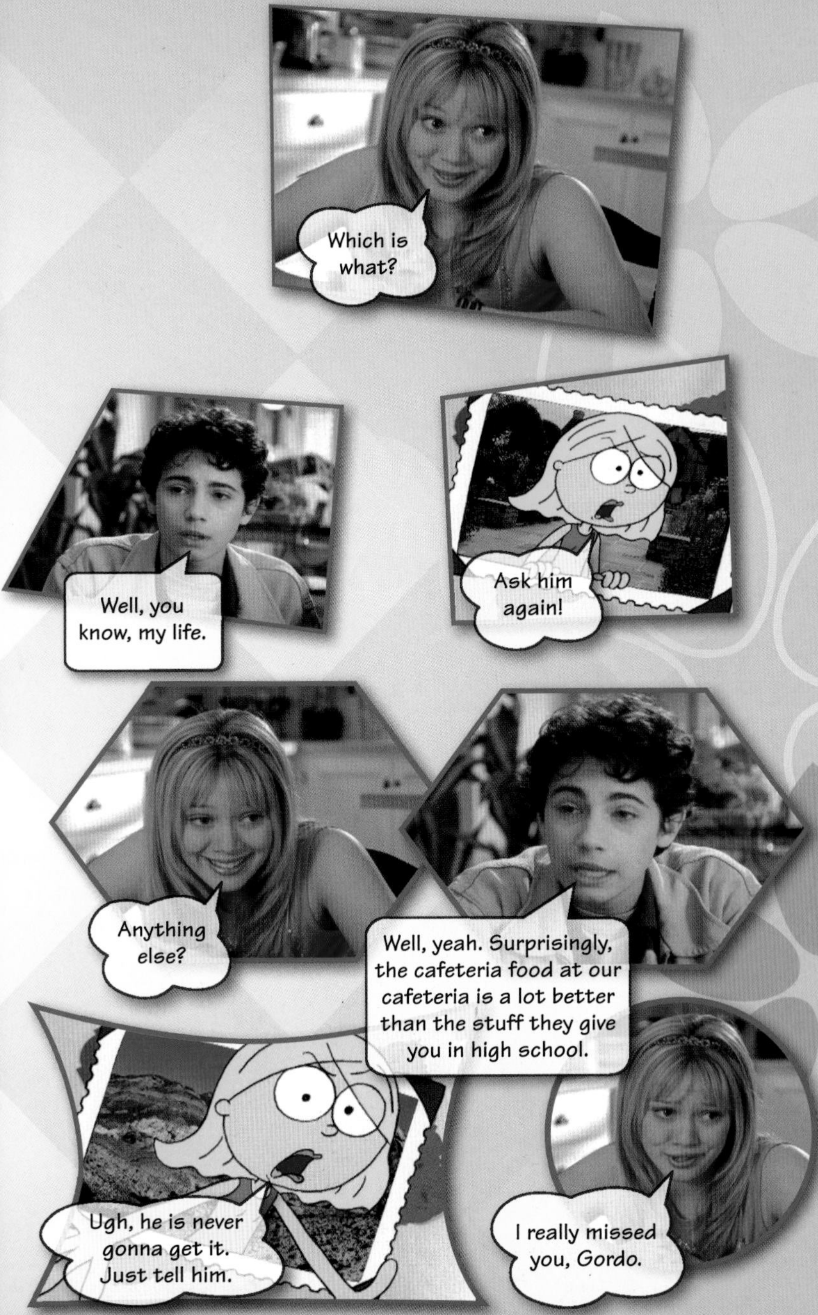
Which is what?
Well, you know, my life.
Ask him again!
Anything else?
Well, yeah. Surprisingly, the cafeteria food at our cafeteria is a lot better than the stuff they give you in high school.
Ugh, he is never gonna get it. Just tell him.
I really missed you, Gordo.

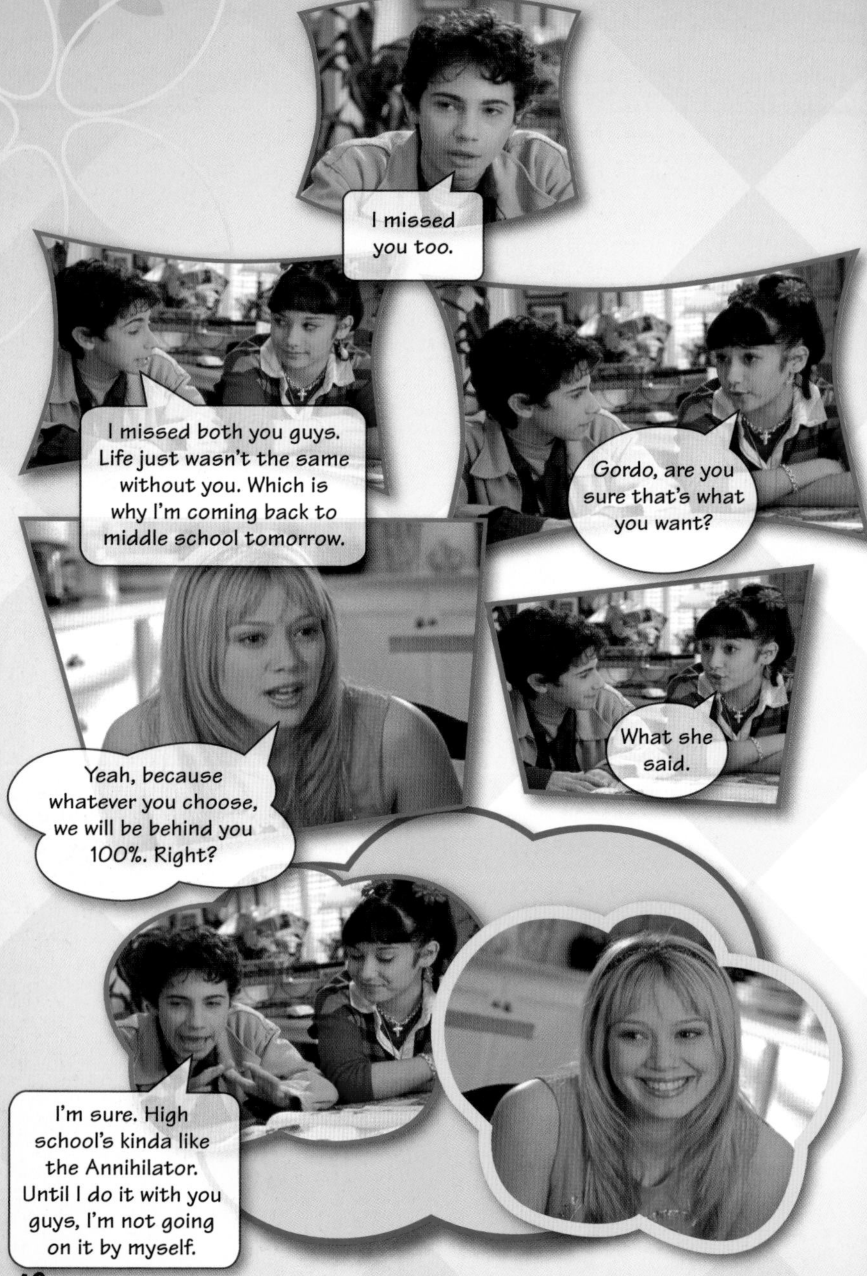
I missed you too.
I missed both you guys. Life just wasn't the same without you. Which is why I'm coming back to middle school tomorrow.
Gordo, are you sure that's what you want?
Yeah, because whatever you choose, we will be behind you 100%. Right?
What she said.
I'm sure. High school's kinda like the Annihilator. Until I do it with you guys, I'm not going on it by myself.

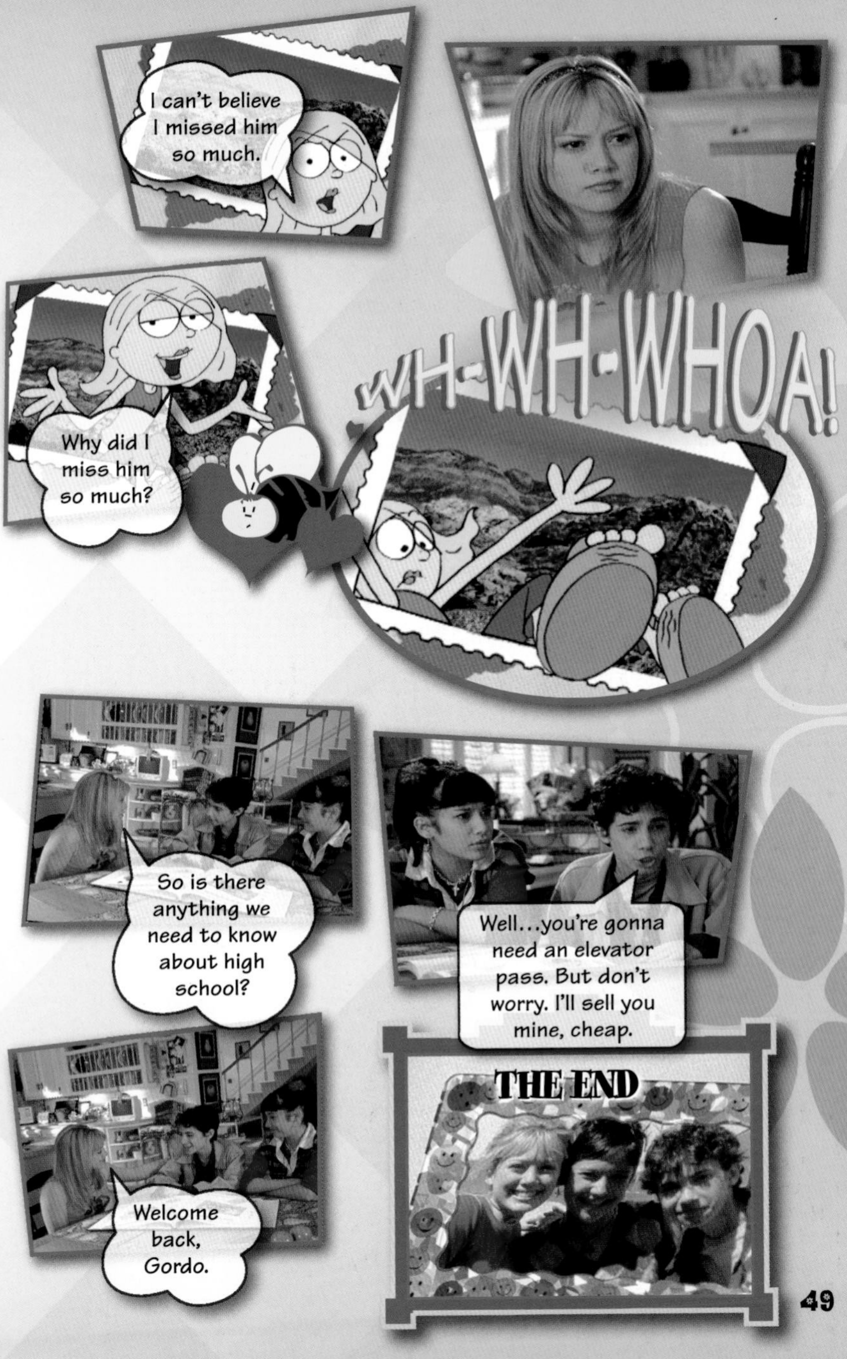
I can't believe I missed him so much.
Why did I miss him so much?
WH-WH-WHOA!
So is there anything we need to know about high school?
Well...you're gonna need an elevator pass. But don't worry. I'll sell you mine, cheap.
Welcome back, Gordo.
THE END

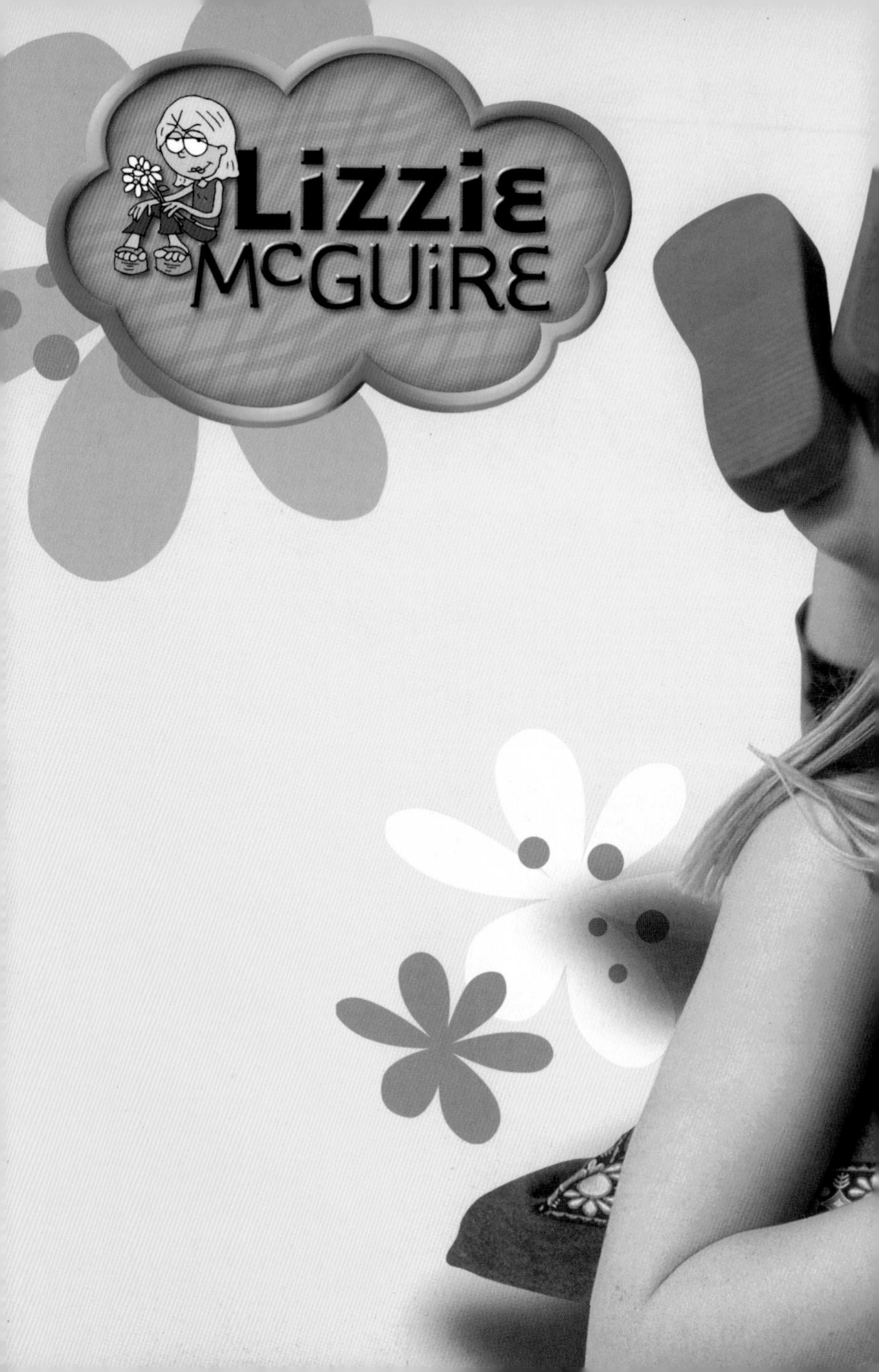
Lizzie
McGuire

Episode 12

"Mom's Best Friend"

A book about mother-daughter relationships inspires Lizzie to make friends with her mom. It's all good as long as they're hanging at the Digital Bean or taking a pottery class after school—but when her mom begins to confide in her, Lizzie realizes she'd rather have a mother than a new best friend.

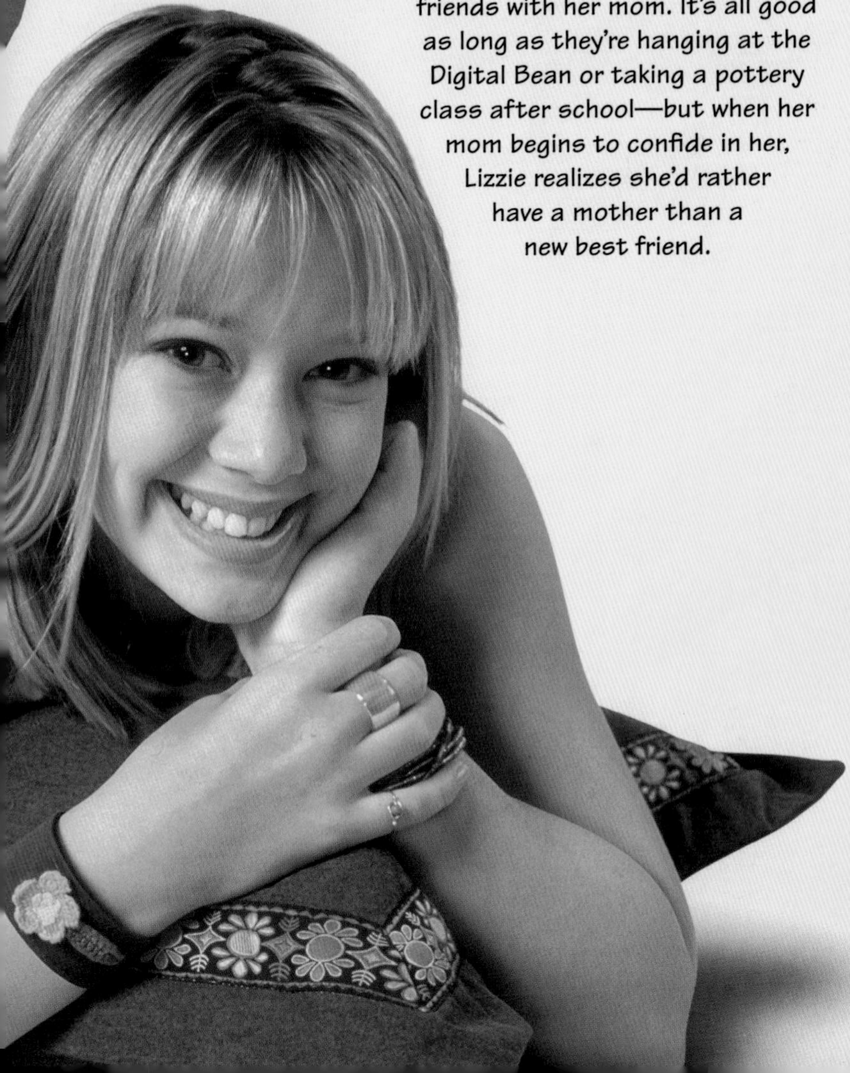

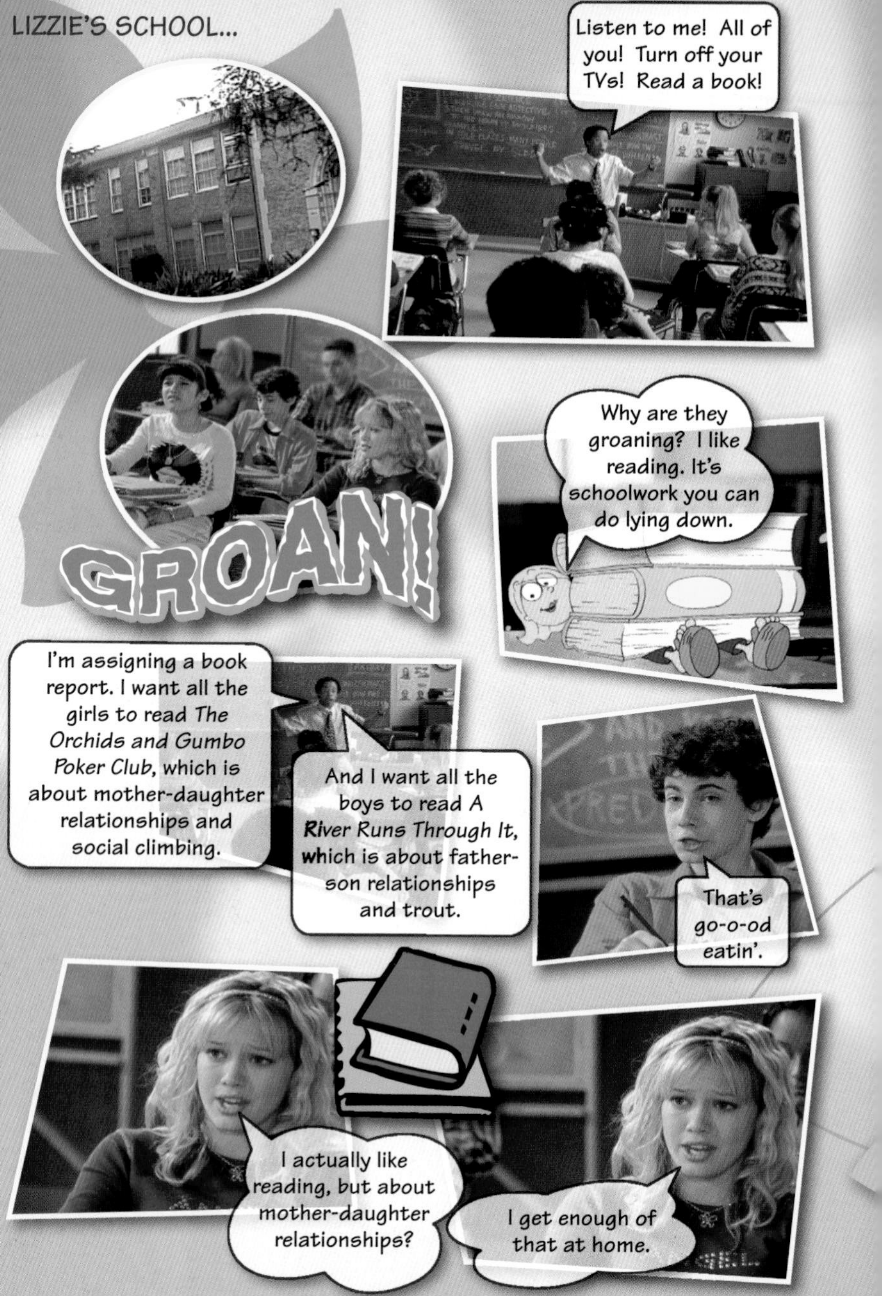
LIZZIE'S SCHOOL...
Listen to me! All of you! Turn off your TVs! Read a book!
GROAN!
Why are they groaning? I like reading. It's schoolwork you can do lying down.
I'm assigning a book report. I want all the girls to read *The Orchids and Gumbo Poker Club*, which is about mother-daughter relationships and social climbing.
And I want all the boys to read *A River Runs Through It*, which is about father-son relationships and trout.
That's go-o-od eatin'.
I actually like reading, but about mother-daughter relationships?
I get enough of that at home.

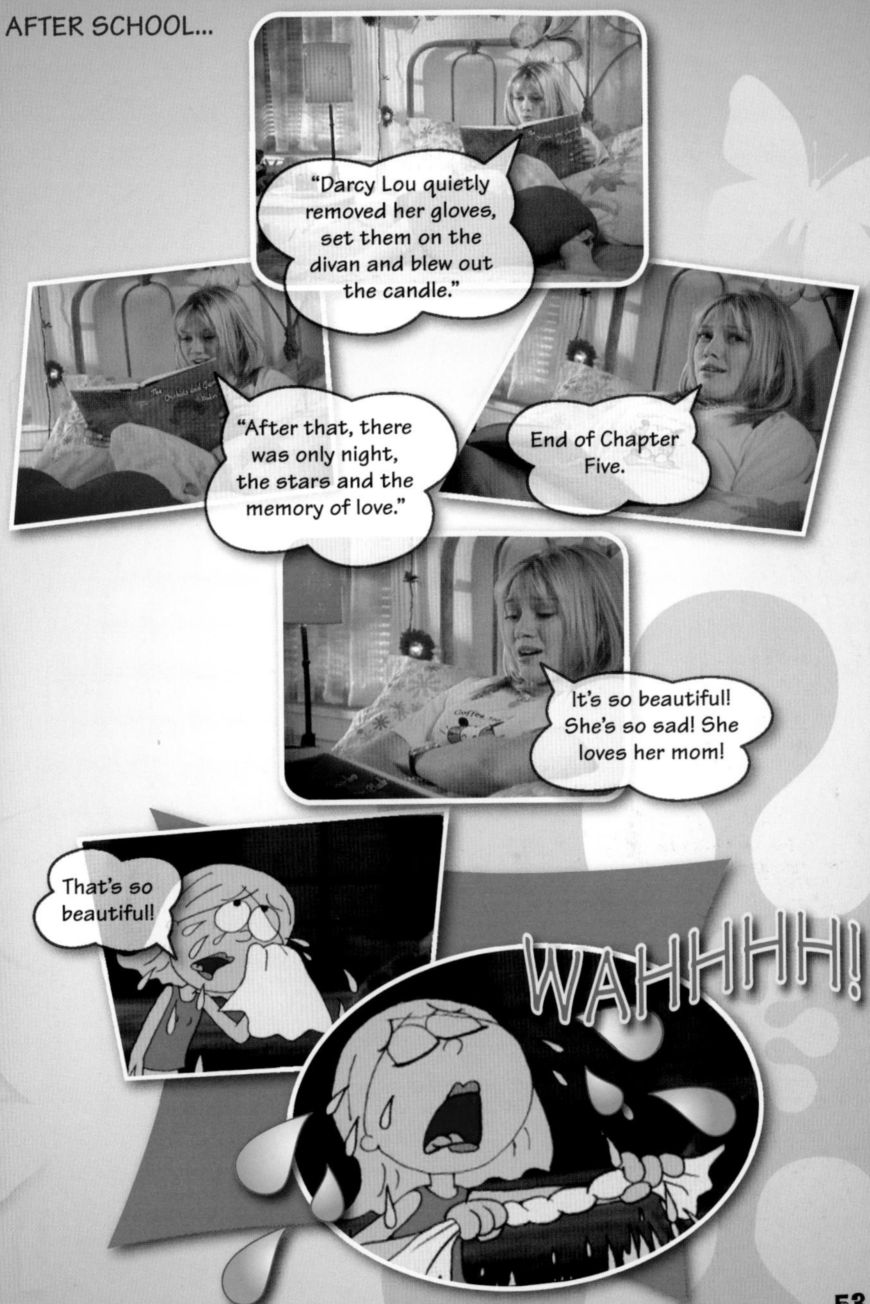
AFTER SCHOOL...
"Darcy Lou quietly removed her gloves, set them on the divan and blew out the candle."
"After that, there was only night, the stars and the memory of love."
End of Chapter Five.
It's so beautiful! She's so sad! She loves her mom!
That's so beautiful!
WAHHHH!

We're in a lull, Lanny. We need to come up with something to do.

HMMM...

You're right. It's the wrong time of the year for rocket-powered skiing.

C'mon, there's gotta be something that we can do. Think... think, think, think...

SPROING!

OOH-HA-HA-HA!

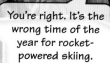

HEE HEE!

Now we've got a chimp. That's something to work with.

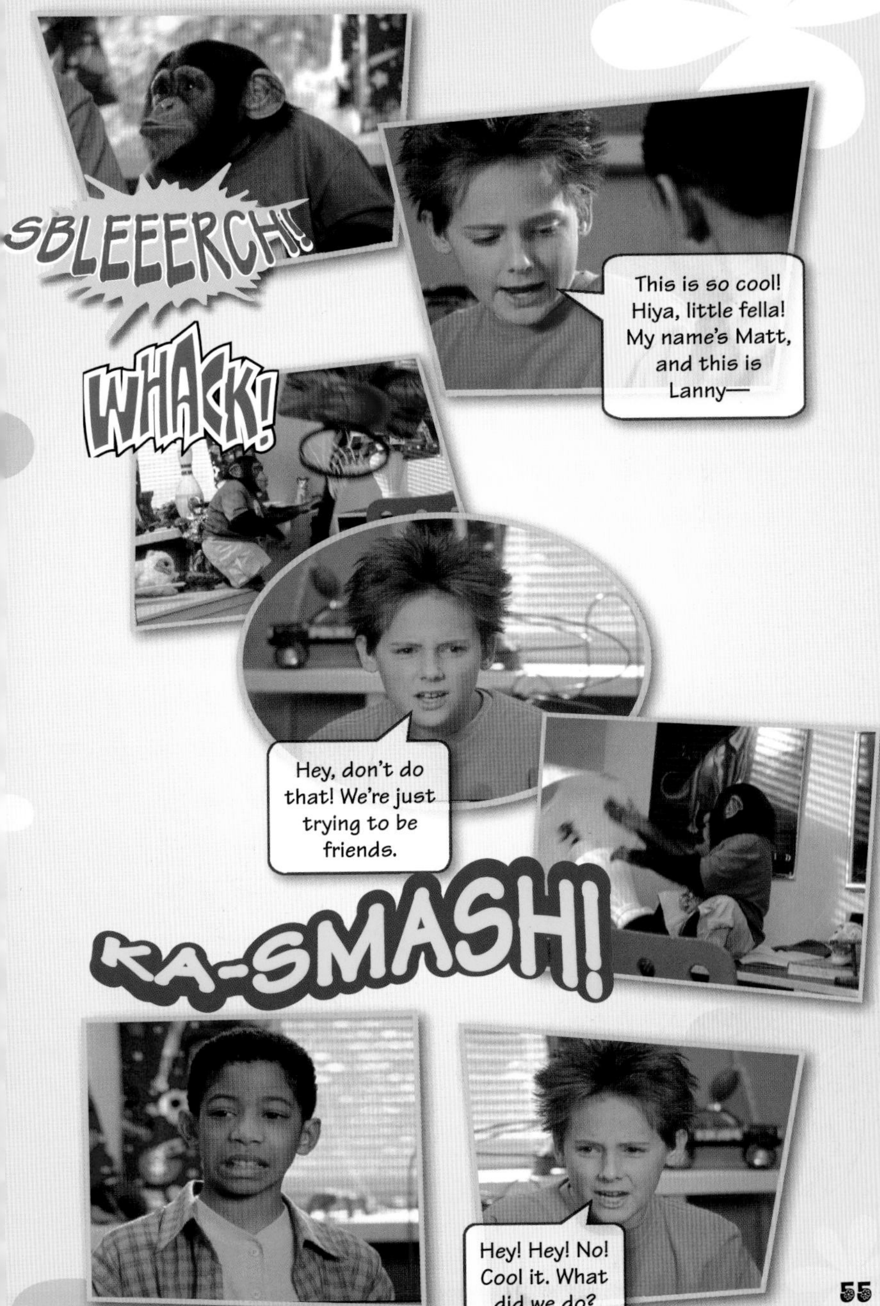
SBLEEERCH!
This is so cool! Hiya, little fella! My name's Matt, and this is Lanny—
WHACK!
Hey, don't do that! We're just trying to be friends.
KA-SMASH!
Hey! Hey! No! Cool it. What did we do?

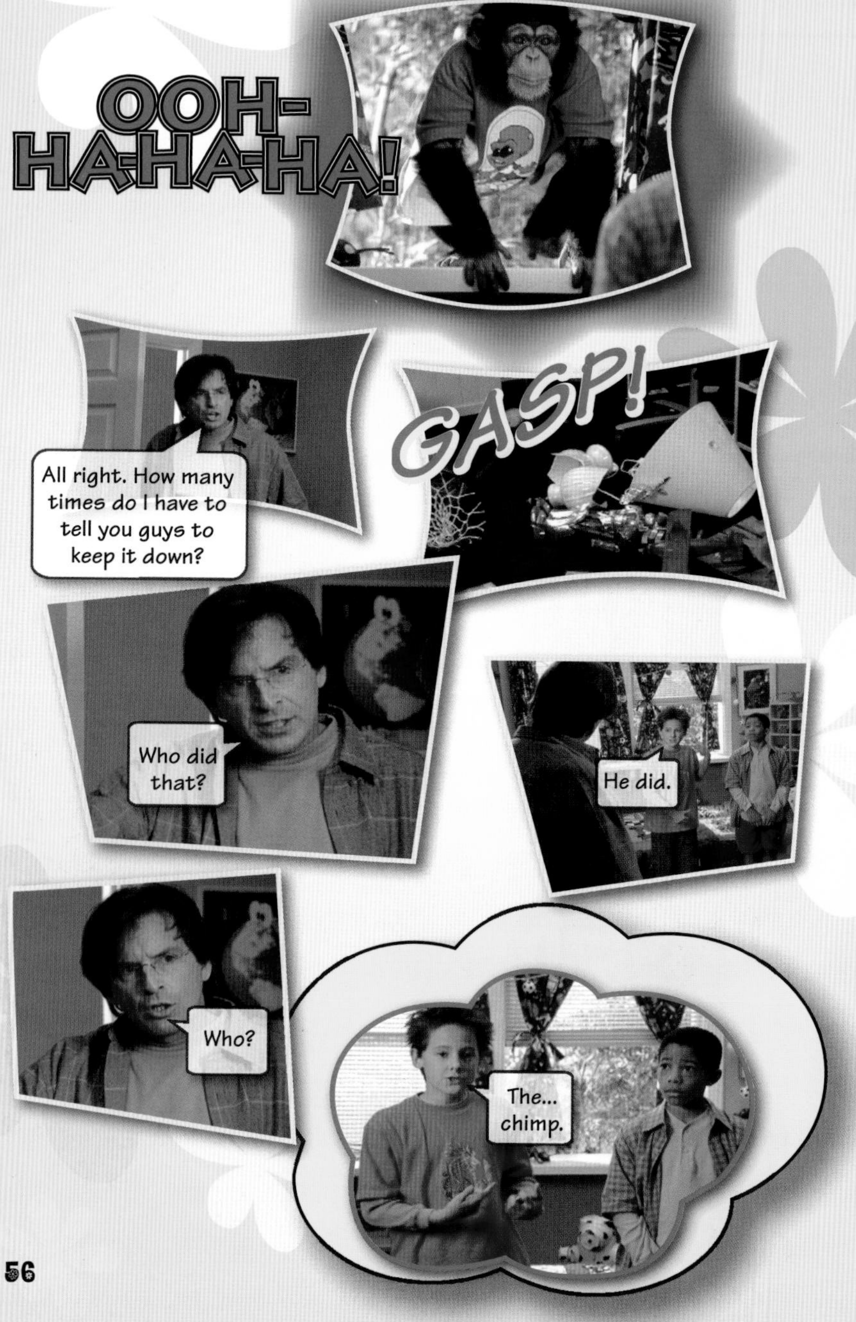
OOH-HA-HA-HA!
All right. How many times do I have to tell you guys to keep it down?
GASP!
Who did that?
He did.
Who?
The... chimp.

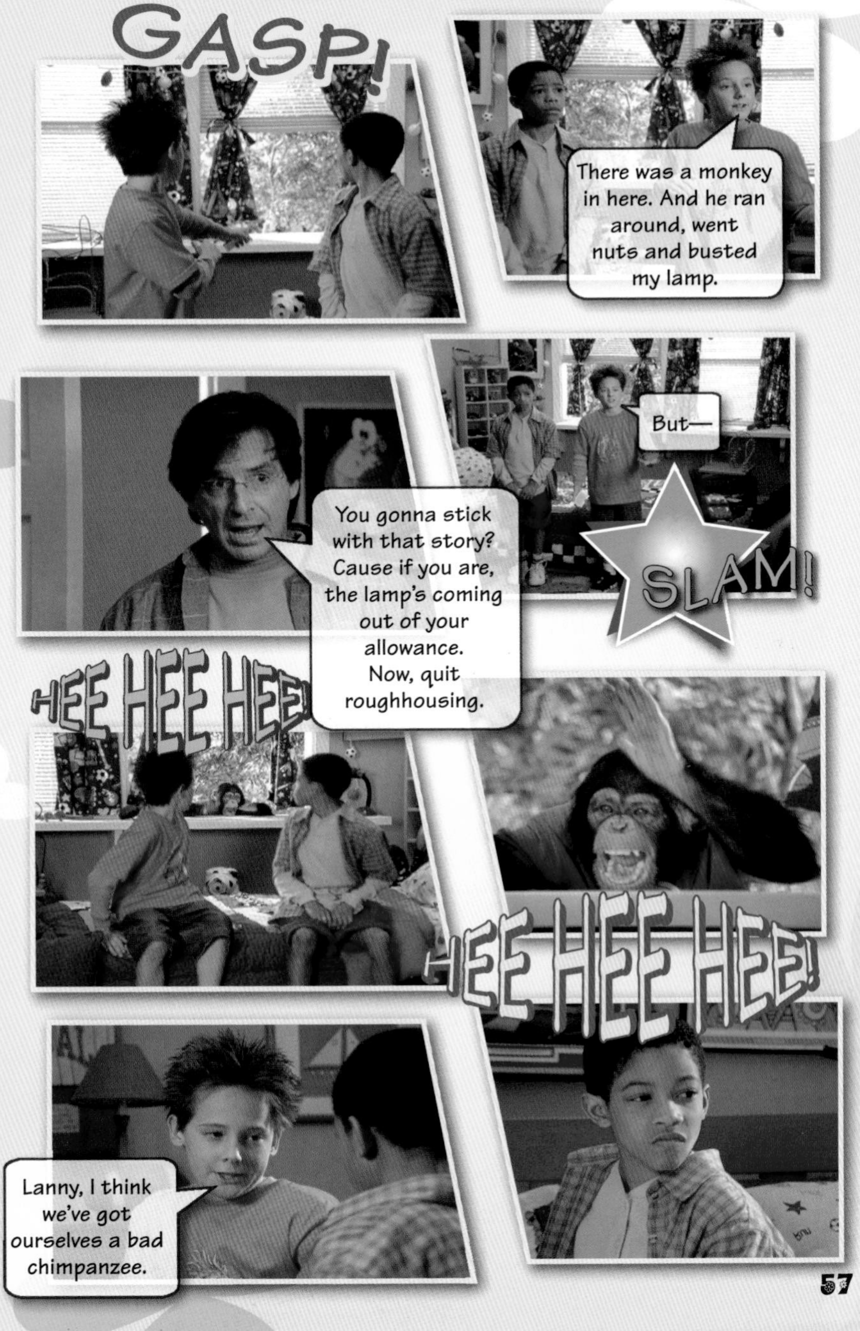
GASP!
There was a monkey in here. And he ran around, went nuts and busted my lamp.
You gonna stick with that story? Cause if you are, the lamp's coming out of your allowance. Now, quit roughhousing.
But—
SLAM!
HEE HEE HEE!
HEE HEE HEE!
Lanny, I think we've got ourselves a bad chimpanzee.

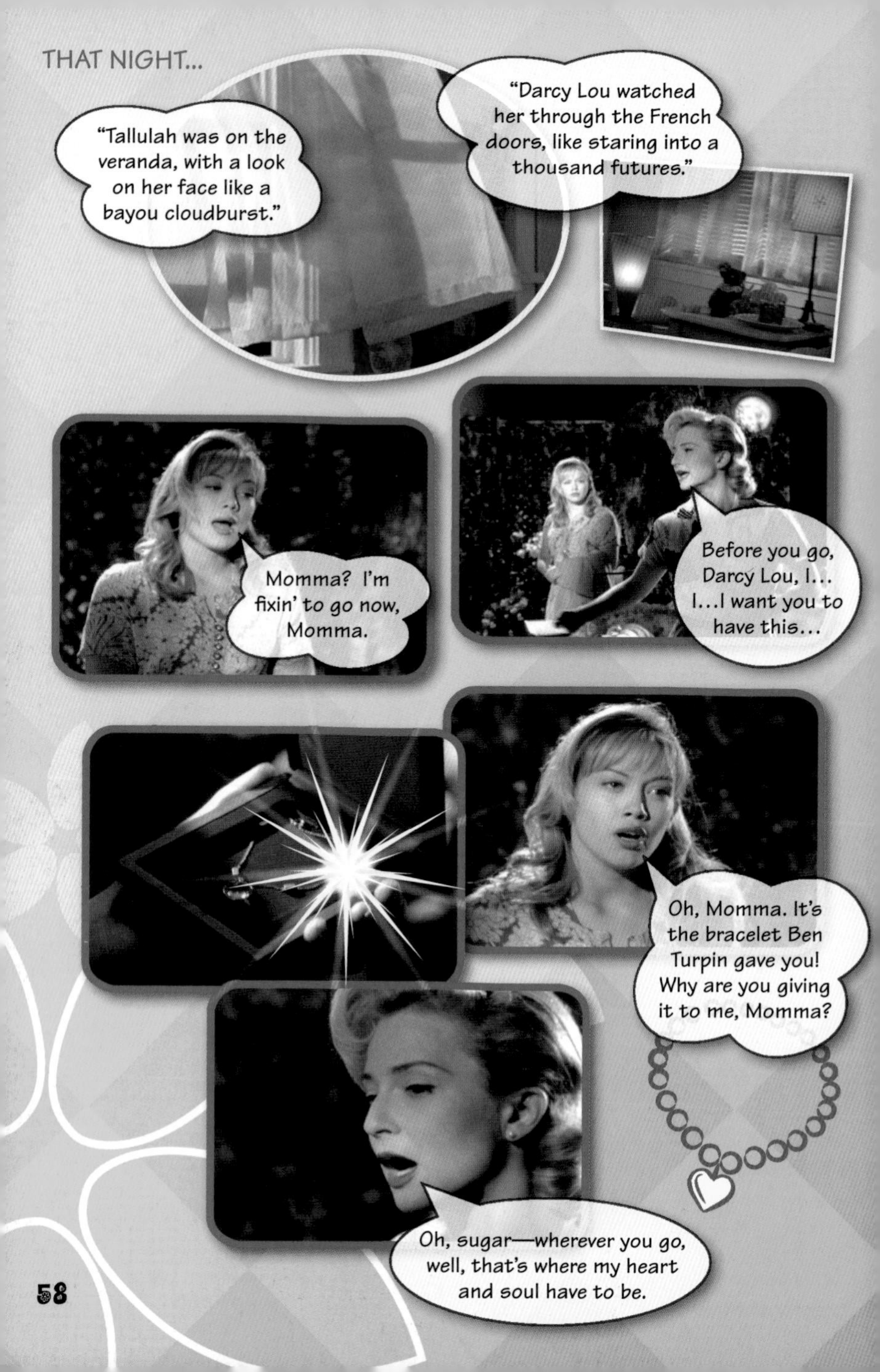
THAT NIGHT...
"Tallulah was on the veranda, with a look on her face like a bayou cloudburst."
"Darcy Lou watched her through the French doors, like staring into a thousand futures."
Momma? I'm fixin' to go now, Momma.
Before you go, Darcy Lou, I... I...I want you to have this...
Oh, Momma. It's the bracelet Ben Turpin gave you! Why are you giving it to me, Momma?
Oh, sugar—wherever you go, well, that's where my heart and soul have to be.

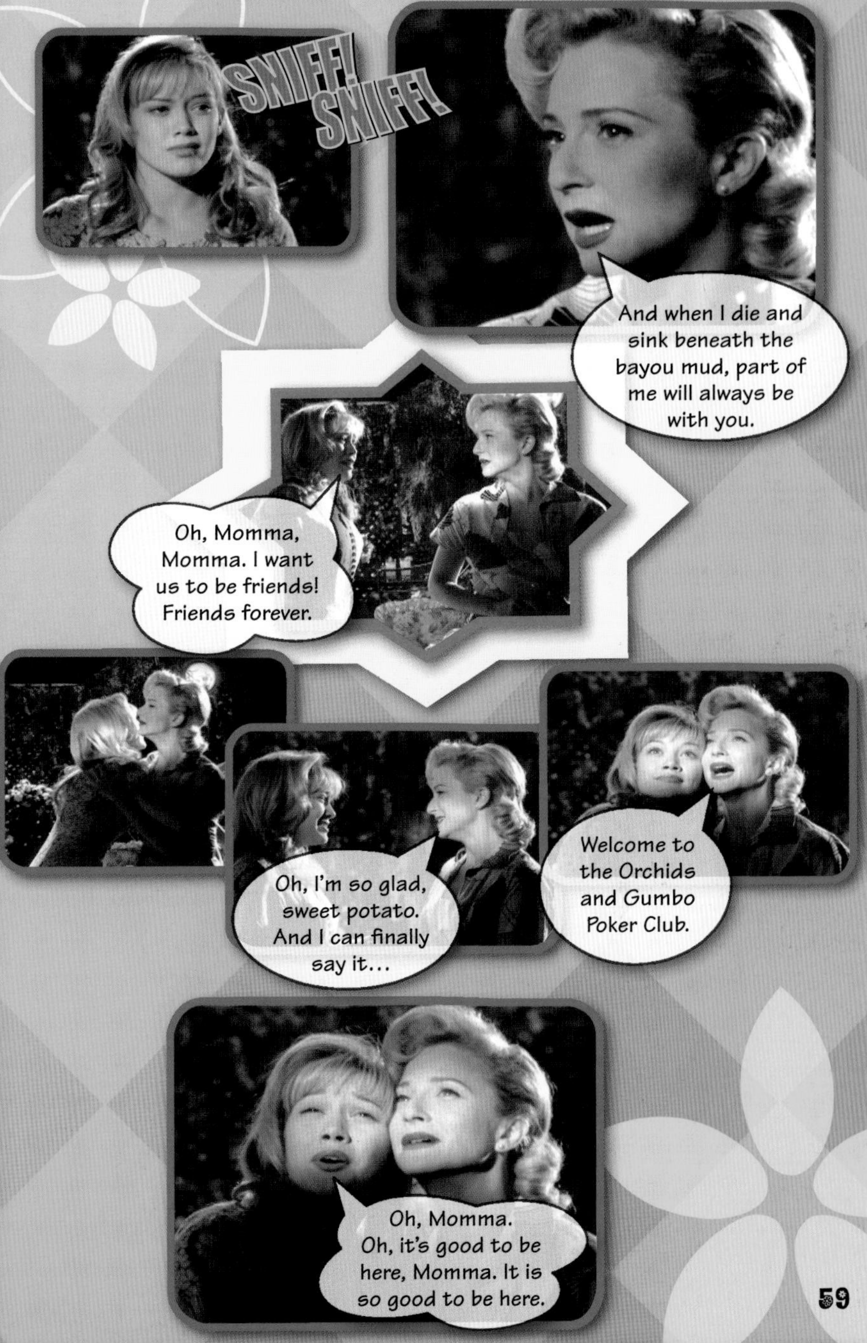
SNIFF! SNIFF!
And when I die and sink beneath the bayou mud, part of me will always be with you.
Oh, Momma, Momma. I want us to be friends! Friends forever.
Oh, I'm so glad, sweet potato. And I can finally say it...
Welcome to the Orchids and Gumbo Poker Club.
Oh, Momma. Oh, it's good to be here, Momma. It is so good to be here.

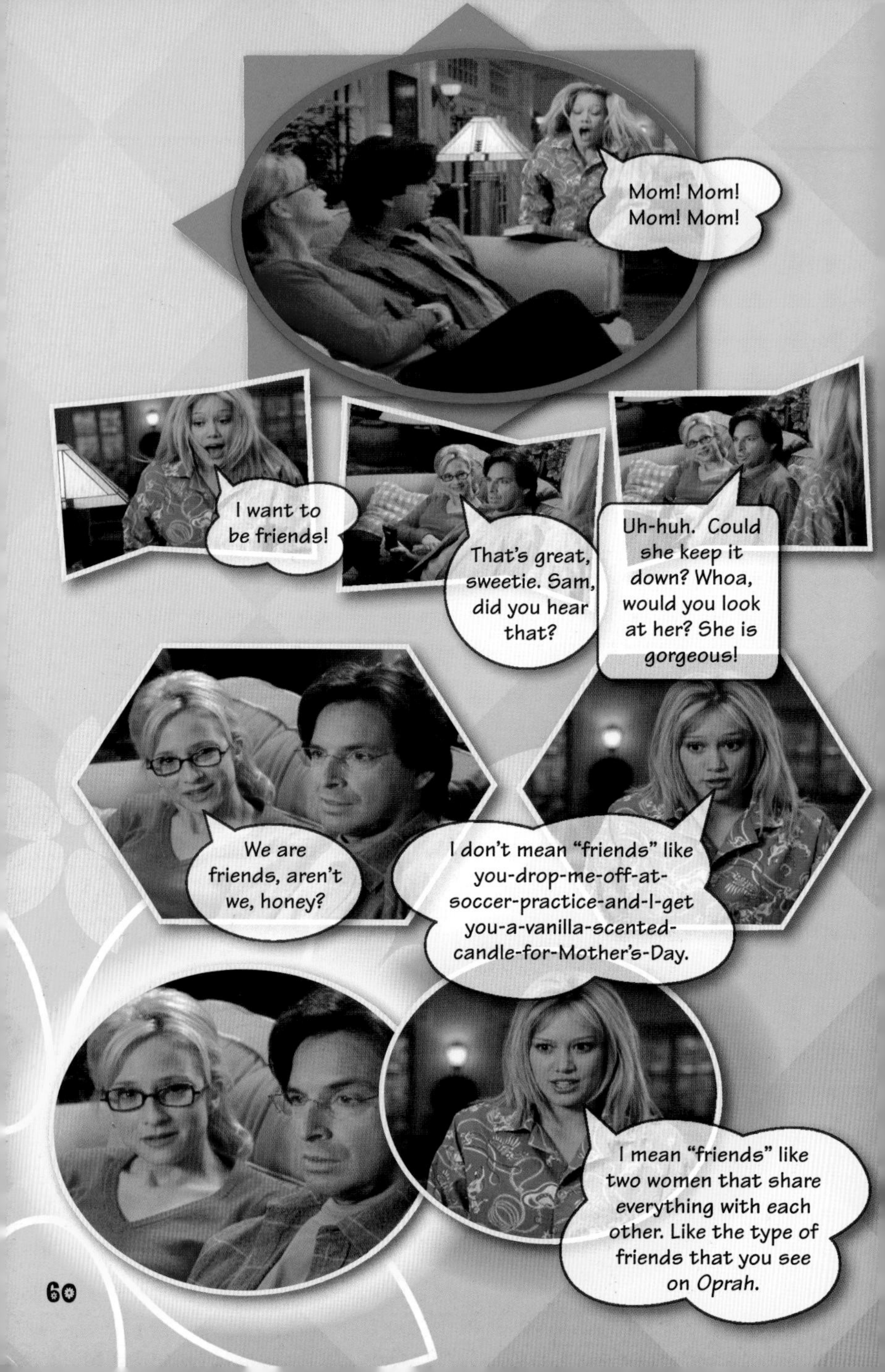
Mom! Mom! Mom! Mom!
I want to be friends!
That's great, sweetie. Sam, did you hear that?
Uh-huh. Could she keep it down? Whoa, would you look at her? She is gorgeous!
We are friends, aren't we, honey?
I don't mean "friends" like you-drop-me-off-at-soccer-practice-and-I-get you-a-vanilla-scented-candle-for-Mother's-Day.
I mean "friends" like two women that share everything with each other. Like the type of friends that you see on *Oprah*.

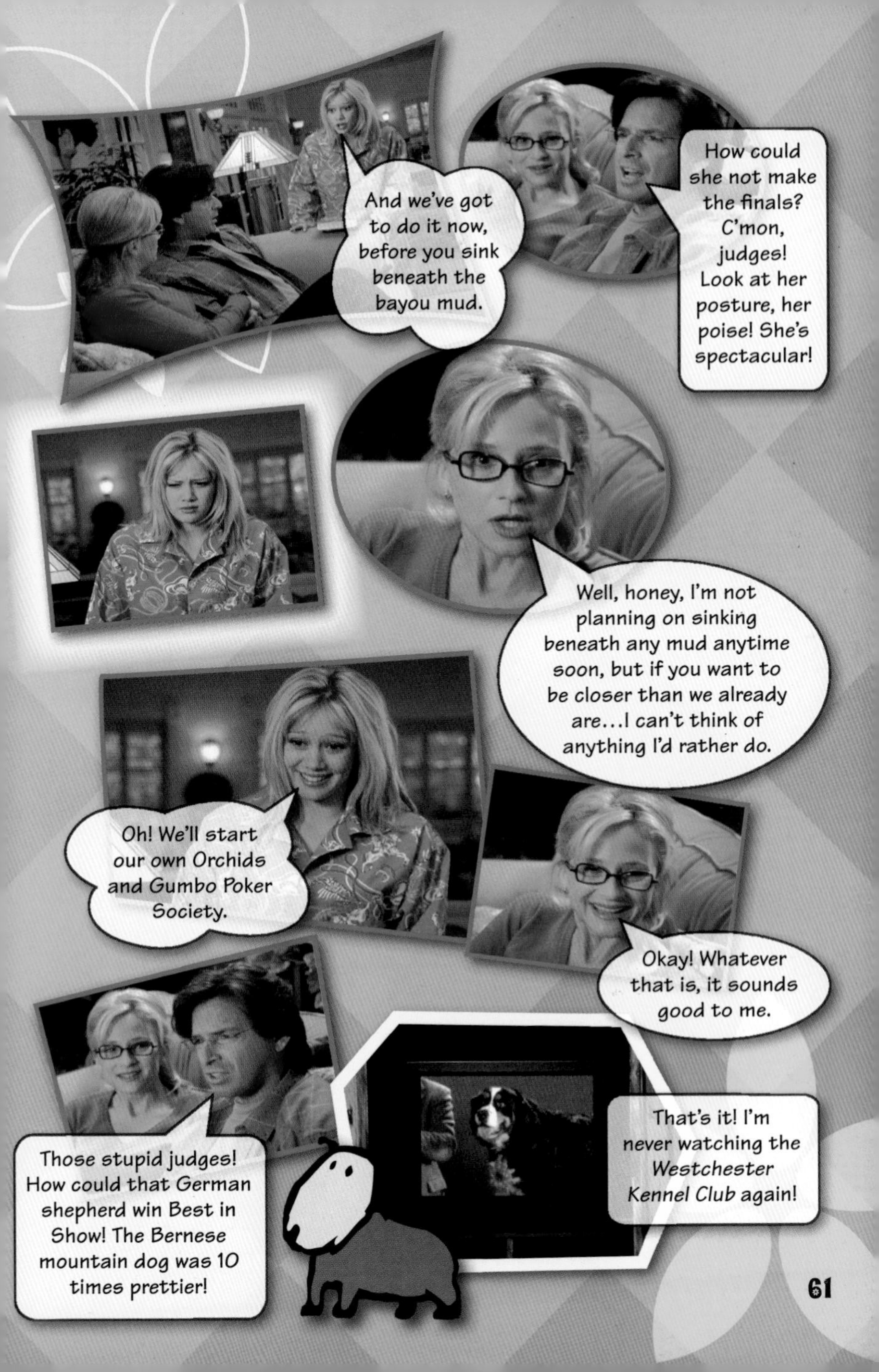
And we've got to do it now, before you sink beneath the bayou mud.
How could she not make the finals? C'mon, judges! Look at her posture, her poise! She's spectacular!
Well, honey, I'm not planning on sinking beneath any mud anytime soon, but if you want to be closer than we already are...I can't think of anything I'd rather do.
Oh! We'll start our own Orchids and Gumbo Poker Society.
Okay! Whatever that is, it sounds good to me.
Those stupid judges! How could that German shepherd win Best in Show! The Bernese mountain dog was 10 times prettier!
That's it! I'm never watching the *Westchester Kennel Club* again!

THE NEXT DAY...

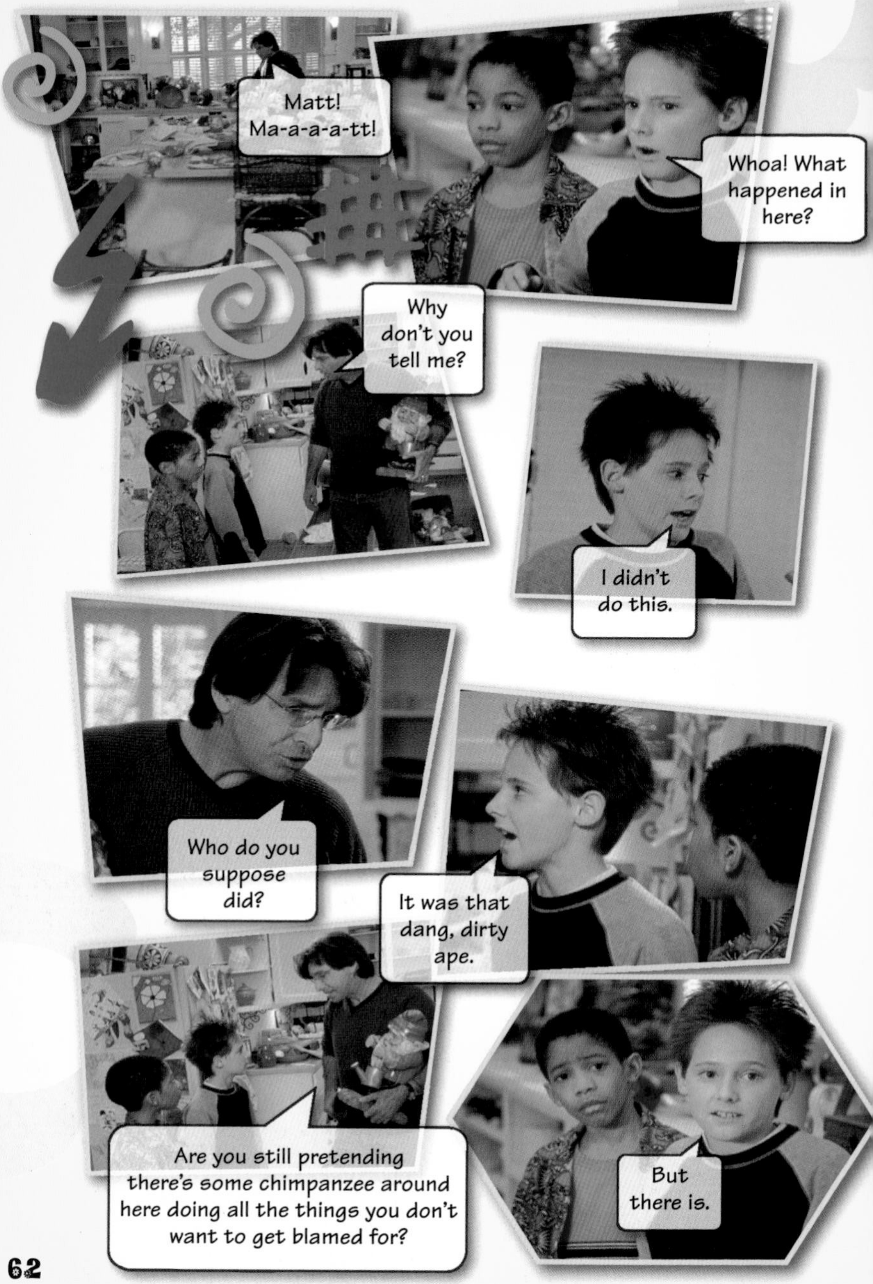
Matt! Ma-a-a-a-tt!
Whoa! What happened in here?
Why don't you tell me?
I didn't do this.
Who do you suppose did?
It was that dang, dirty ape.
Are you still pretending there's some chimpanzee around here doing all the things you don't want to get blamed for?
But there is.

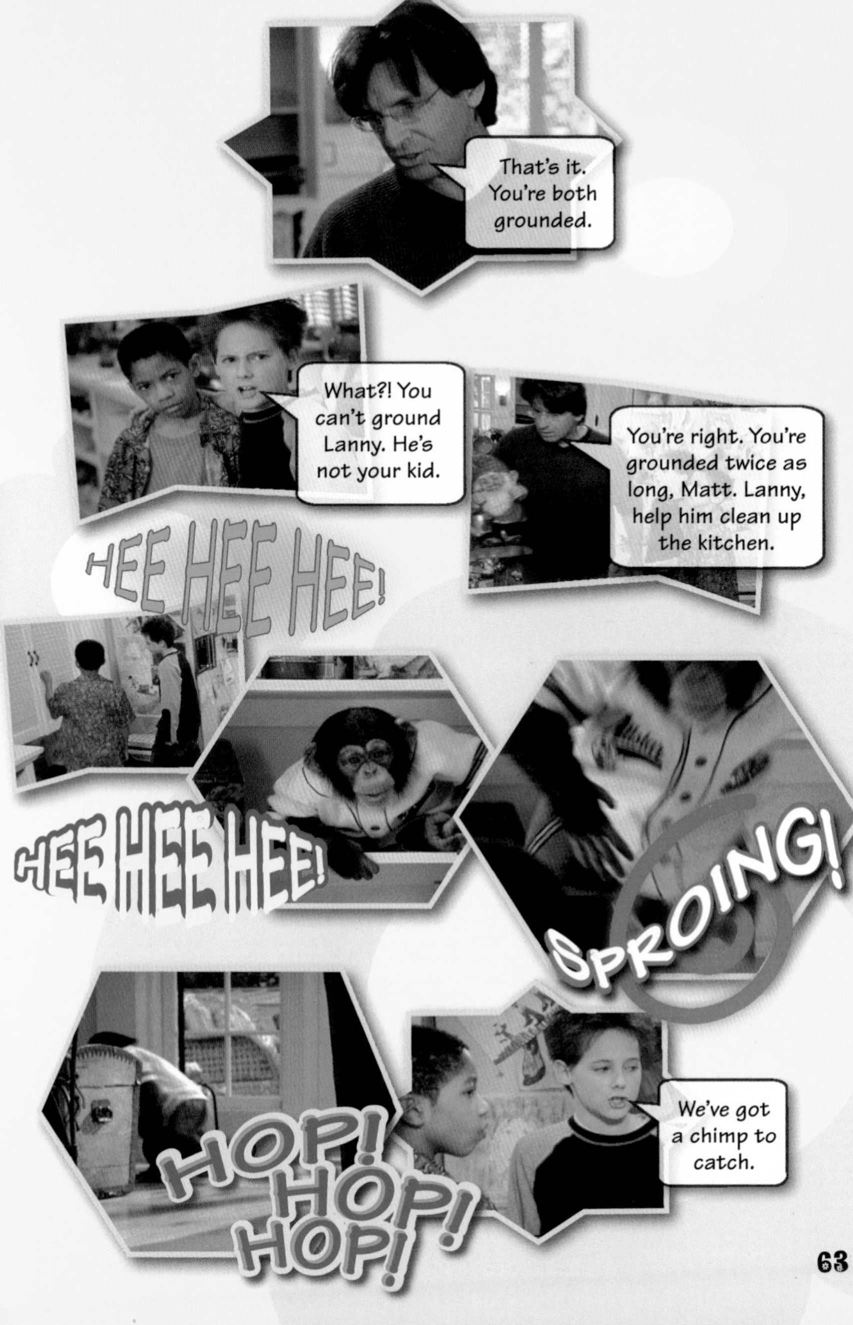
That's it. You're both grounded.
What?! You can't ground Lanny. He's not your kid.
You're right. You're grounded twice as long, Matt. Lanny, help him clean up the kitchen.
HEE HEE HEE!
HEE HEE HEE!
SPROING!
HOP! HOP! HOP!
We've got a chimp to catch.

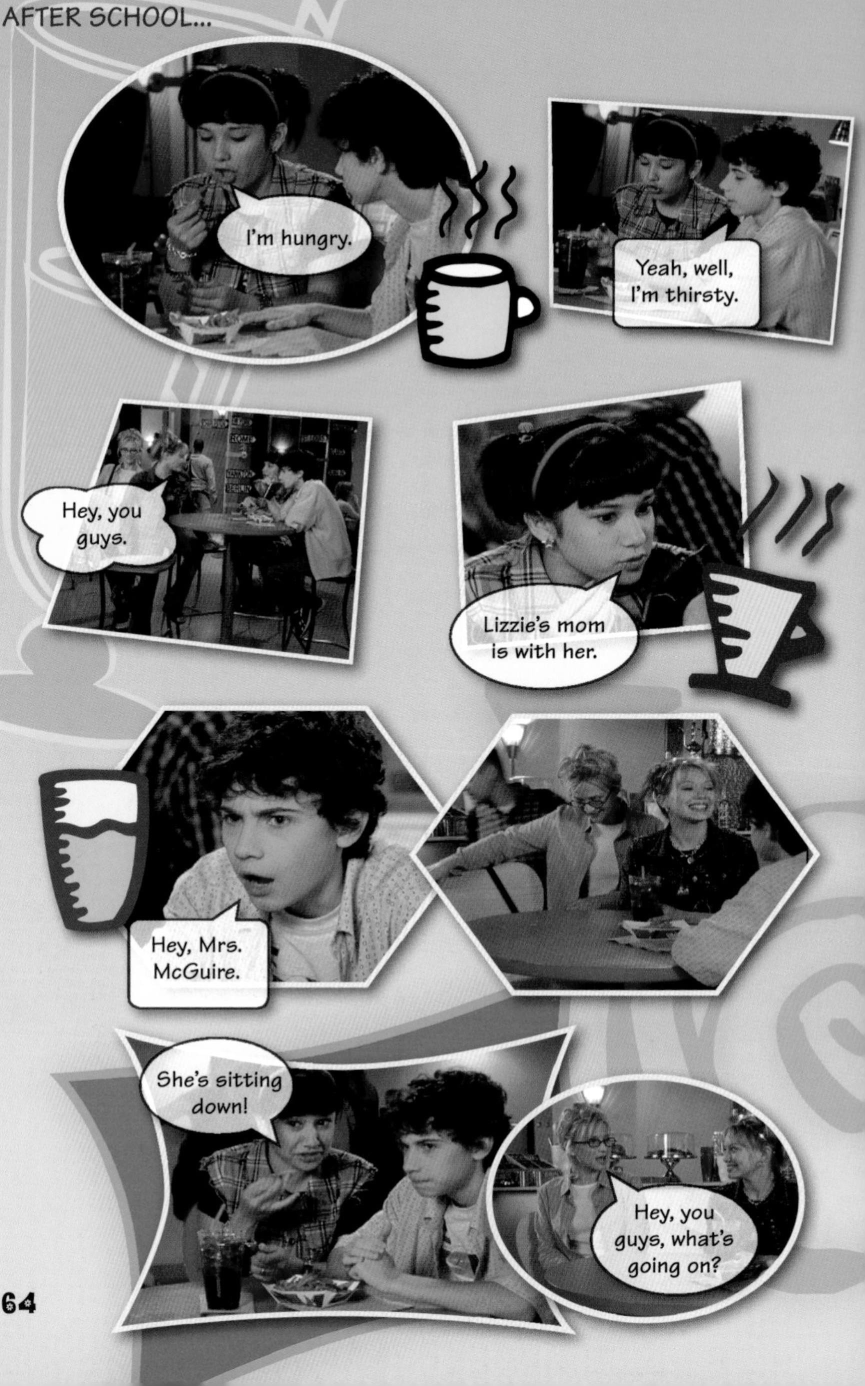
AFTER SCHOOL...
I'm hungry.
Yeah, well, I'm thirsty.
Hey, you guys.
Lizzie's mom is with her.
Hey, Mrs. McGuire.
She's sitting down!
Hey, you guys, what's going on?

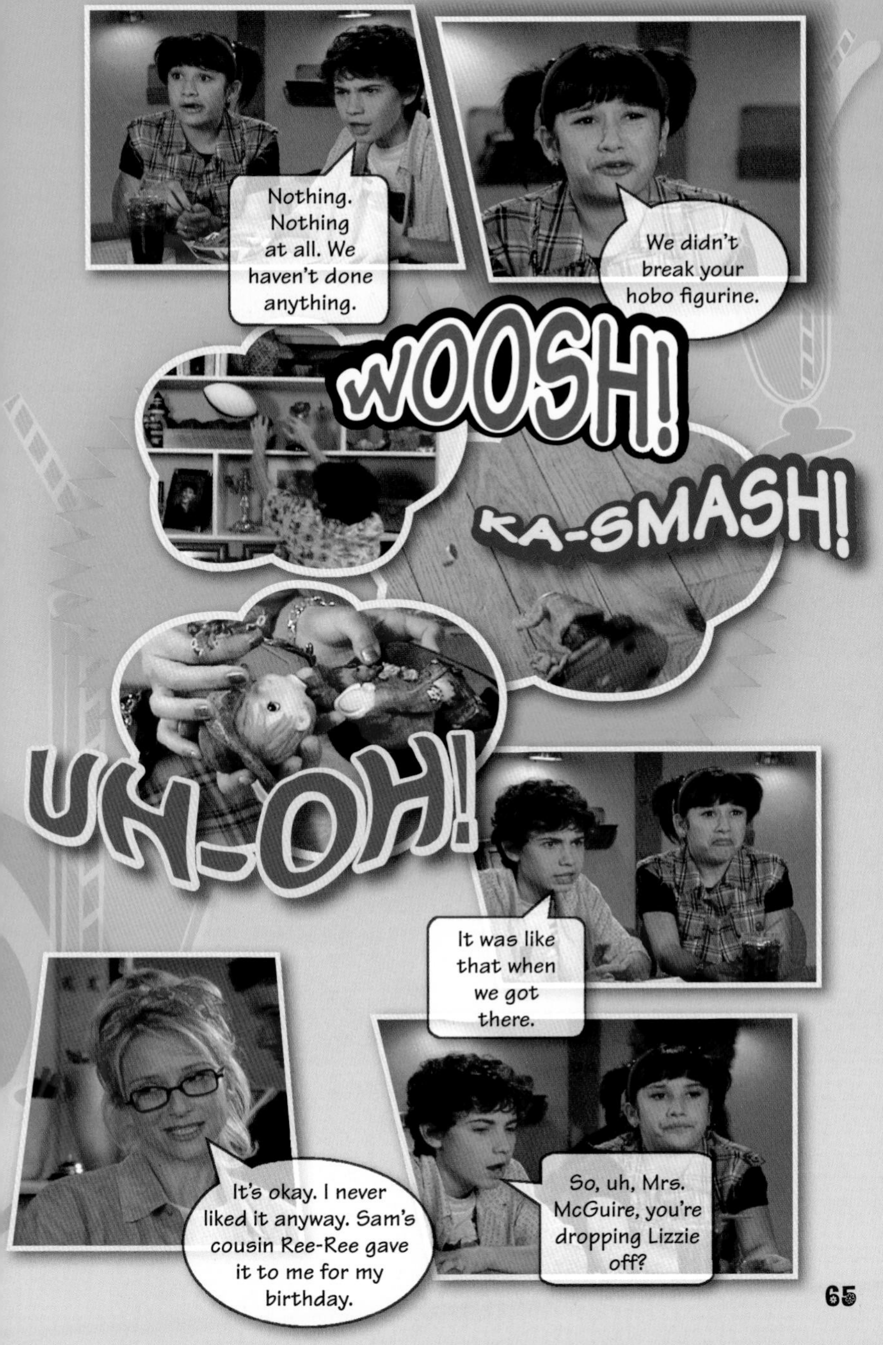

Nothing. Nothing at all. We haven't done anything.
We didn't break your hobo figurine.
WOOSH!
KA-SMASH!
UH-OH!
It was like that when we got there.
It's okay. I never liked it anyway. Sam's cousin Ree-Ree gave it to me for my birthday.
So, uh, Mrs. McGuire, you're dropping Lizzie off?

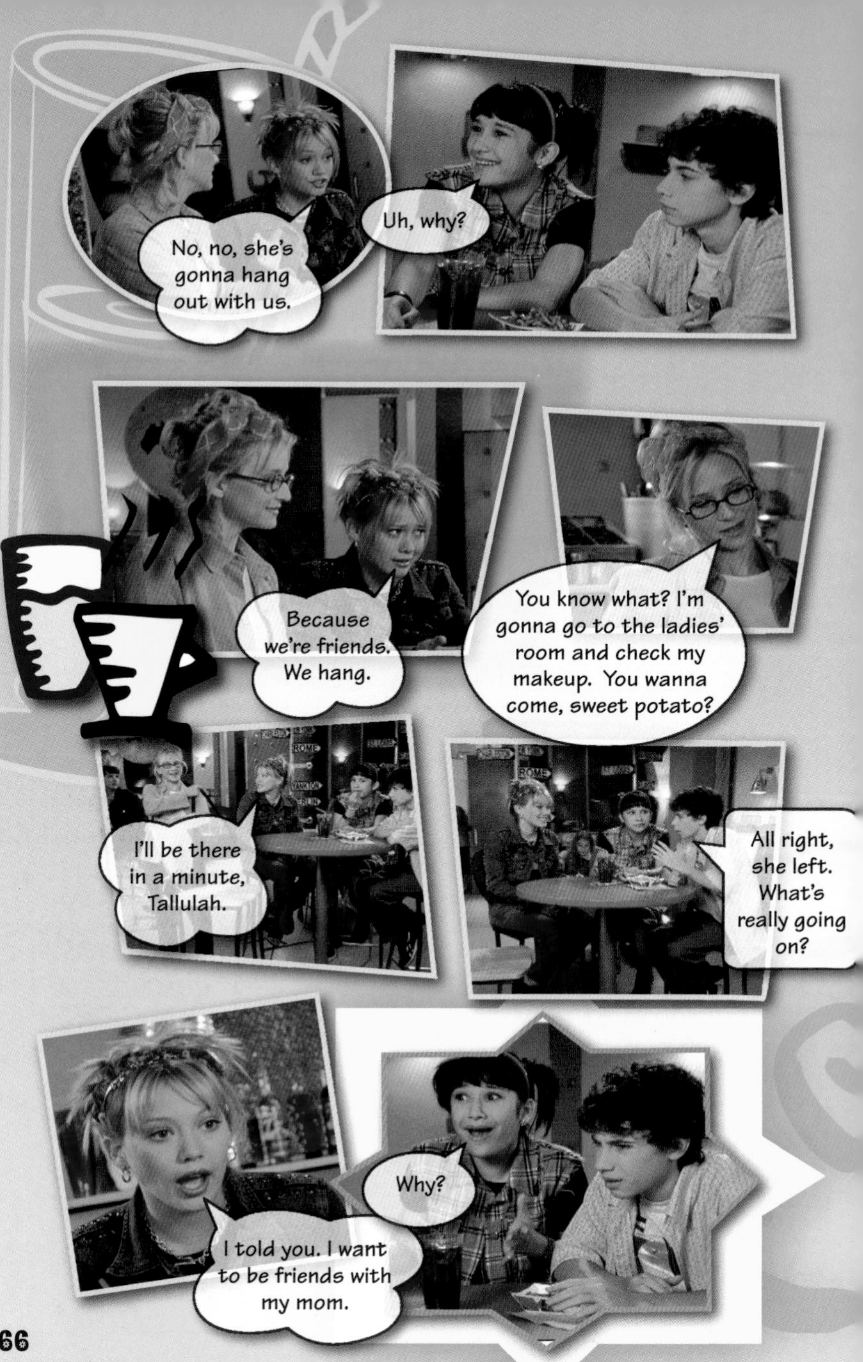
No, no, she's gonna hang out with us.
Uh, why?
Because we're friends. We hang.
You know what? I'm gonna go to the ladies' room and check my makeup. You wanna come, sweet potato?
I'll be there in a minute, Tallulah.
All right, she left. What's really going on?
Why?
I told you. I want to be friends with my mom.

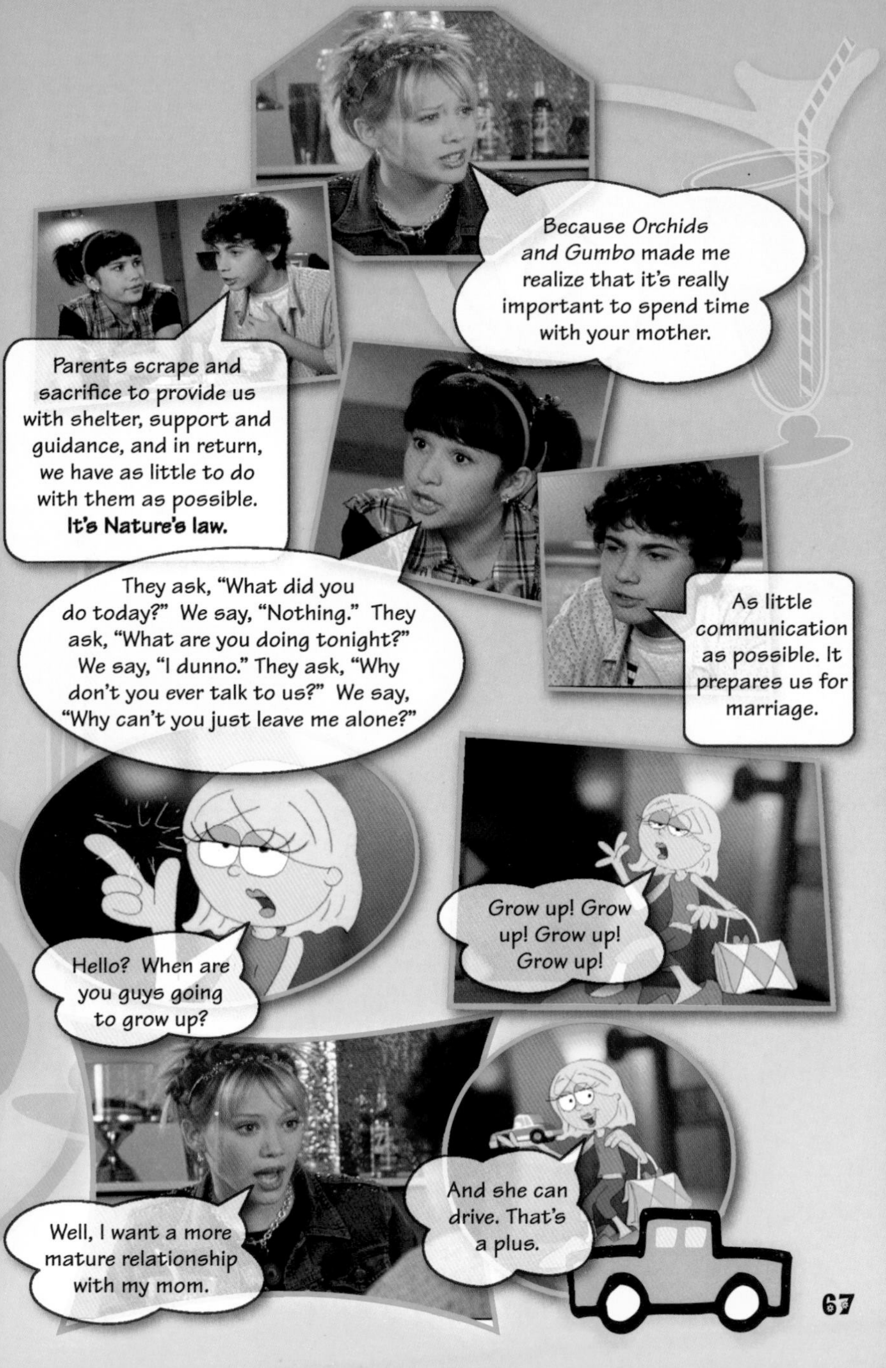
Because *Orchids and Gumbo* made me realize that it's really important to spend time with your mother.
Parents scrape and sacrifice to provide us with shelter, support and guidance, and in return, we have as little to do with them as possible. **It's Nature's law.**
They ask, "What did you do today?" We say, "Nothing." They ask, "What are you doing tonight?" We say, "I dunno." They ask, "Why don't you ever talk to us?" We say, "Why can't you just leave me alone?"
As little communication as possible. It prepares us for marriage.
Hello? When are you guys going to grow up?
Grow up! Grow up! Grow up! Grow up!
Well, I want a more mature relationship with my mom.
And she can drive. That's a plus.

THE NEXT DAY...

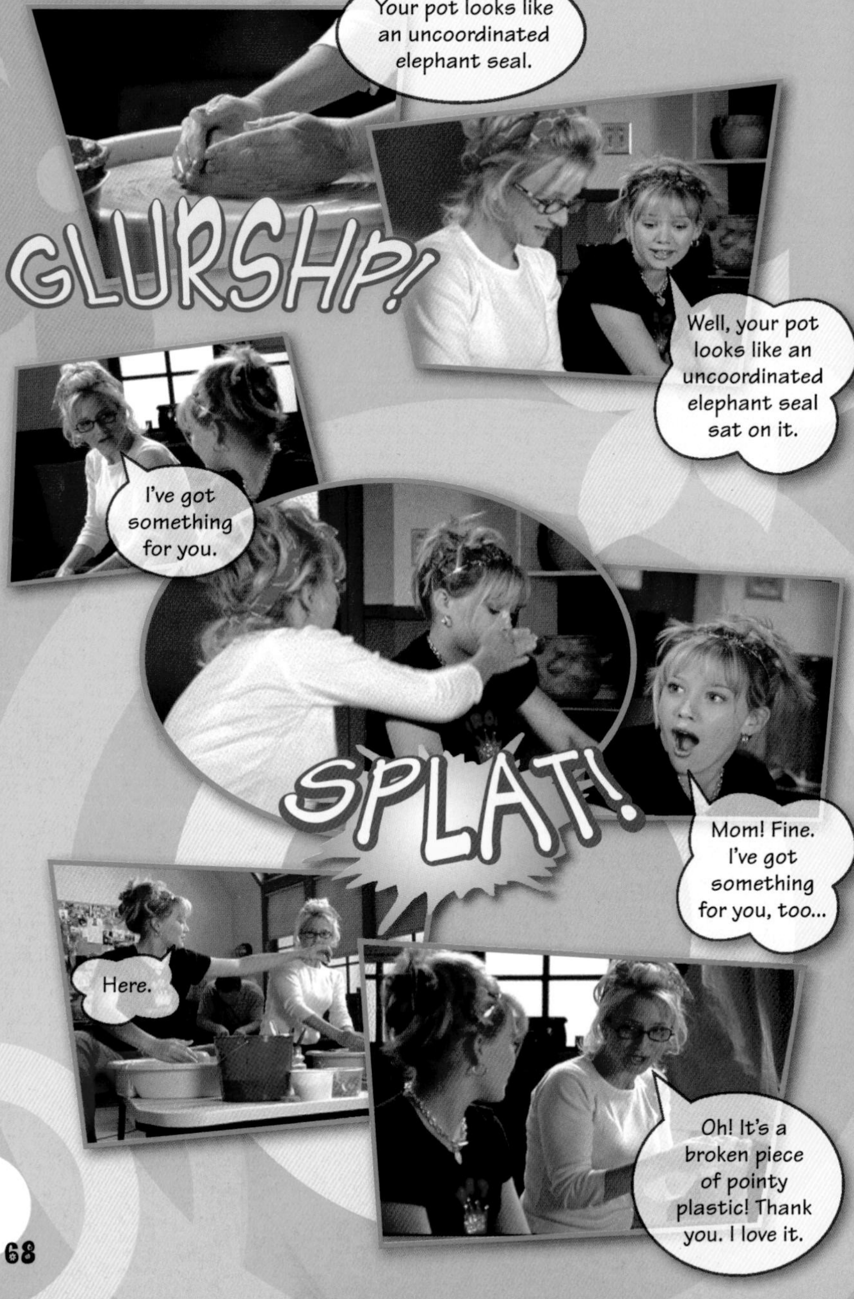
Your pot looks like an uncoordinated elephant seal.
GLURSHP!
Well, your pot looks like an uncoordinated elephant seal sat on it.
I've got something for you.
SPLAT!
Mom! Fine. I've got something for you, too...
Here.
Oh! It's a broken piece of pointy plastic! Thank you. I love it.

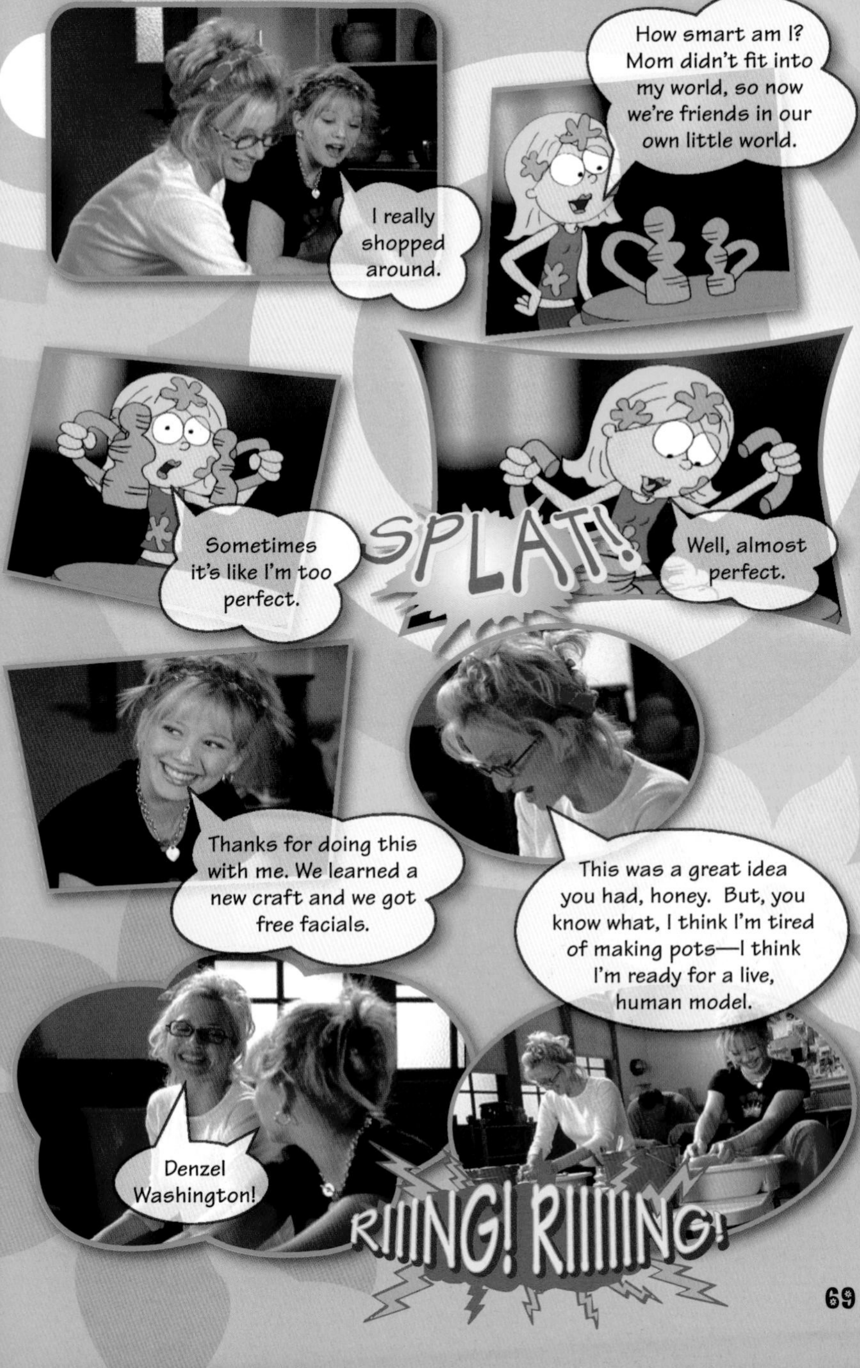
I really shopped around.
How smart am I? Mom didn't fit into my world, so now we're friends in our own little world.
Sometimes it's like I'm too perfect.
SPLAT!
Well, almost perfect.
Thanks for doing this with me. We learned a new craft and we got free facials.
This was a great idea you had, honey. But, you know what, I think I'm tired of making pots—I think I'm ready for a live, human model.
Denzel Washington!
RIIING! RIIIING!

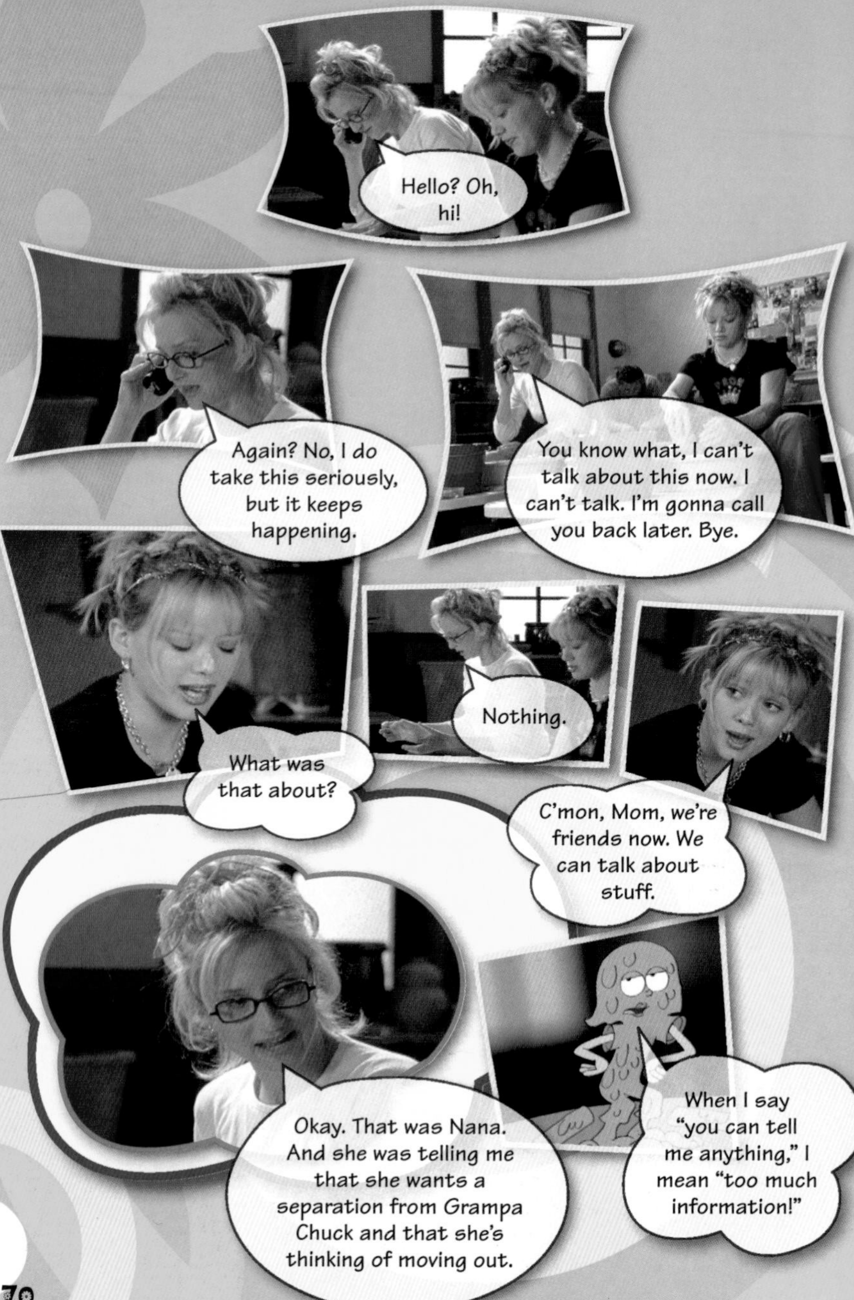
Hello? Oh, hi!
Again? No, I do take this seriously, but it keeps happening.
You know what, I can't talk about this now. I can't talk. I'm gonna call you back later. Bye.
What was that about?
Nothing.
C'mon, Mom, we're friends now. We can talk about stuff.
Okay. That was Nana. And she was telling me that she wants a separation from Grampa Chuck and that she's thinking of moving out.
When I say "you can tell me anything," I mean "too much information!"

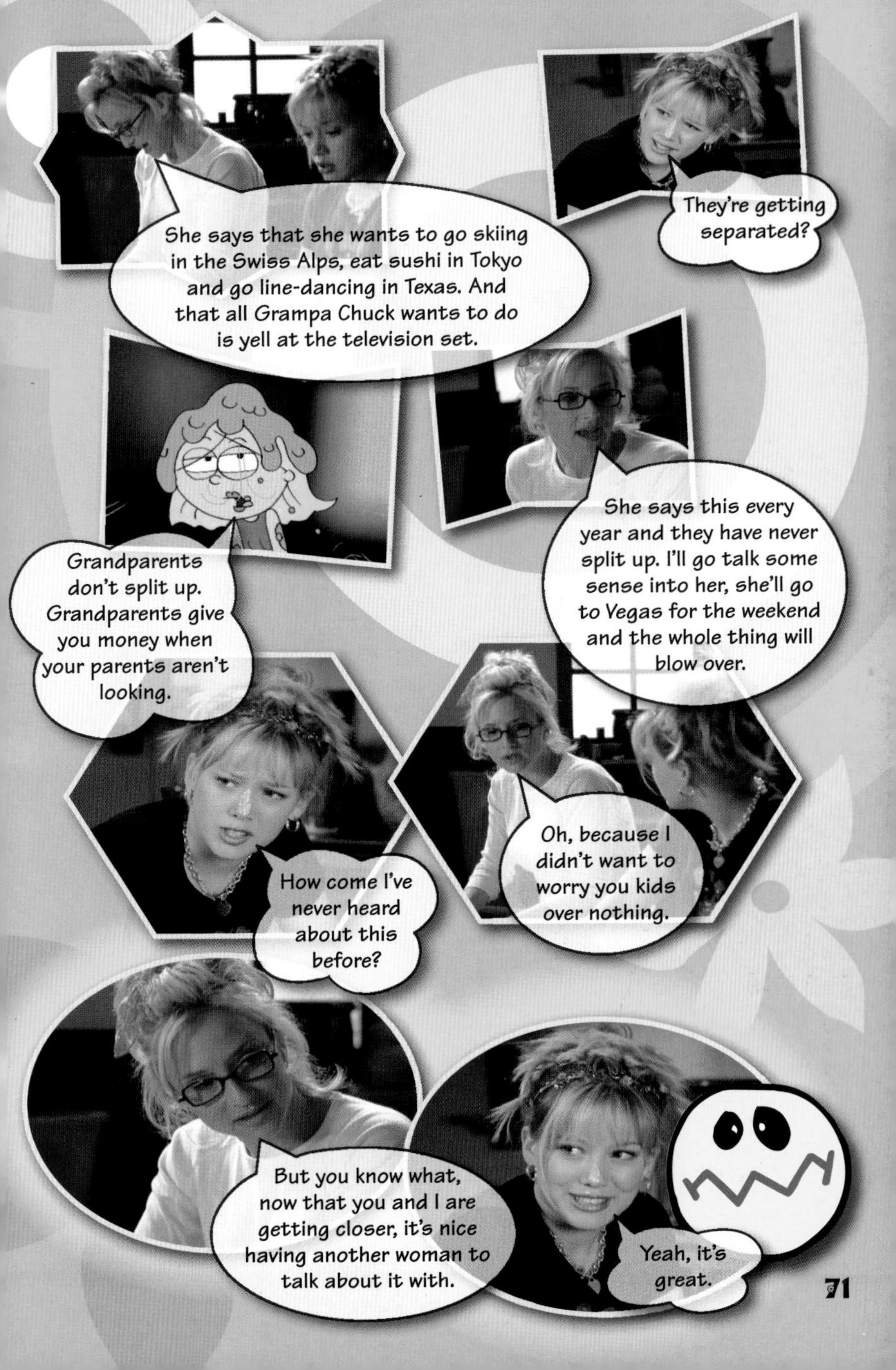
She says that she wants to go skiing in the Swiss Alps, eat sushi in Tokyo and go line-dancing in Texas. And that all Grampa Chuck wants to do is yell at the television set.
They're getting separated?
Grandparents don't split up. Grandparents give you money when your parents aren't looking.
She says this every year and they have never split up. I'll go talk some sense into her, she'll go to Vegas for the weekend and the whole thing will blow over.
How come I've never heard about this before?
Oh, because I didn't want to worry you kids over nothing.
But you know what, now that you and I are getting closer, it's nice having another woman to talk about it with.
Yeah, it's great.

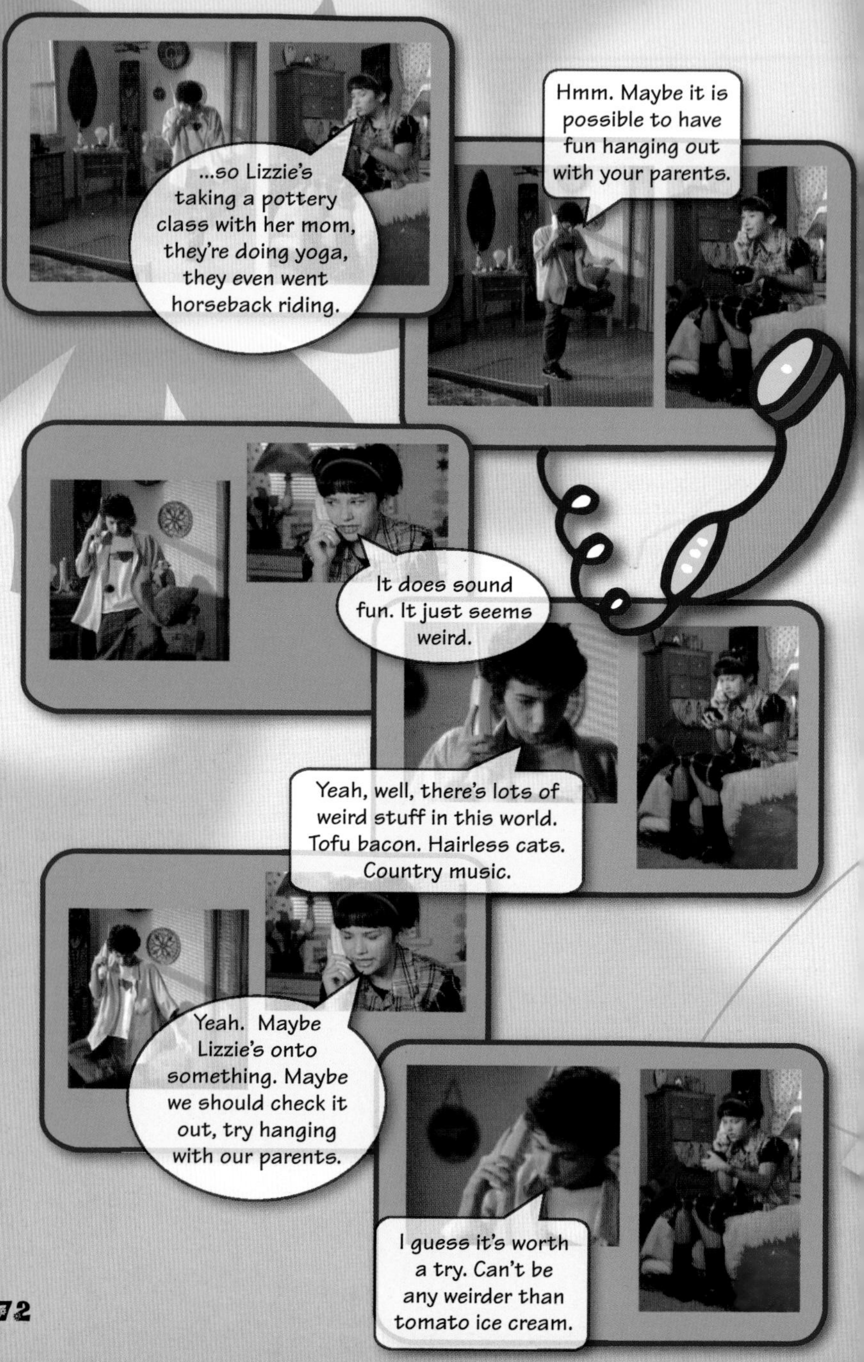
...so Lizzie's taking a pottery class with her mom, they're doing yoga, they even went horseback riding.
Hmm. Maybe it is possible to have fun hanging out with your parents.
It does sound fun. It just seems weird.
Yeah, well, there's lots of weird stuff in this world. Tofu bacon. Hairless cats. Country music.
Yeah. Maybe Lizzie's onto something. Maybe we should check it out, try hanging with our parents.
I guess it's worth a try. Can't be any weirder than tomato ice cream.

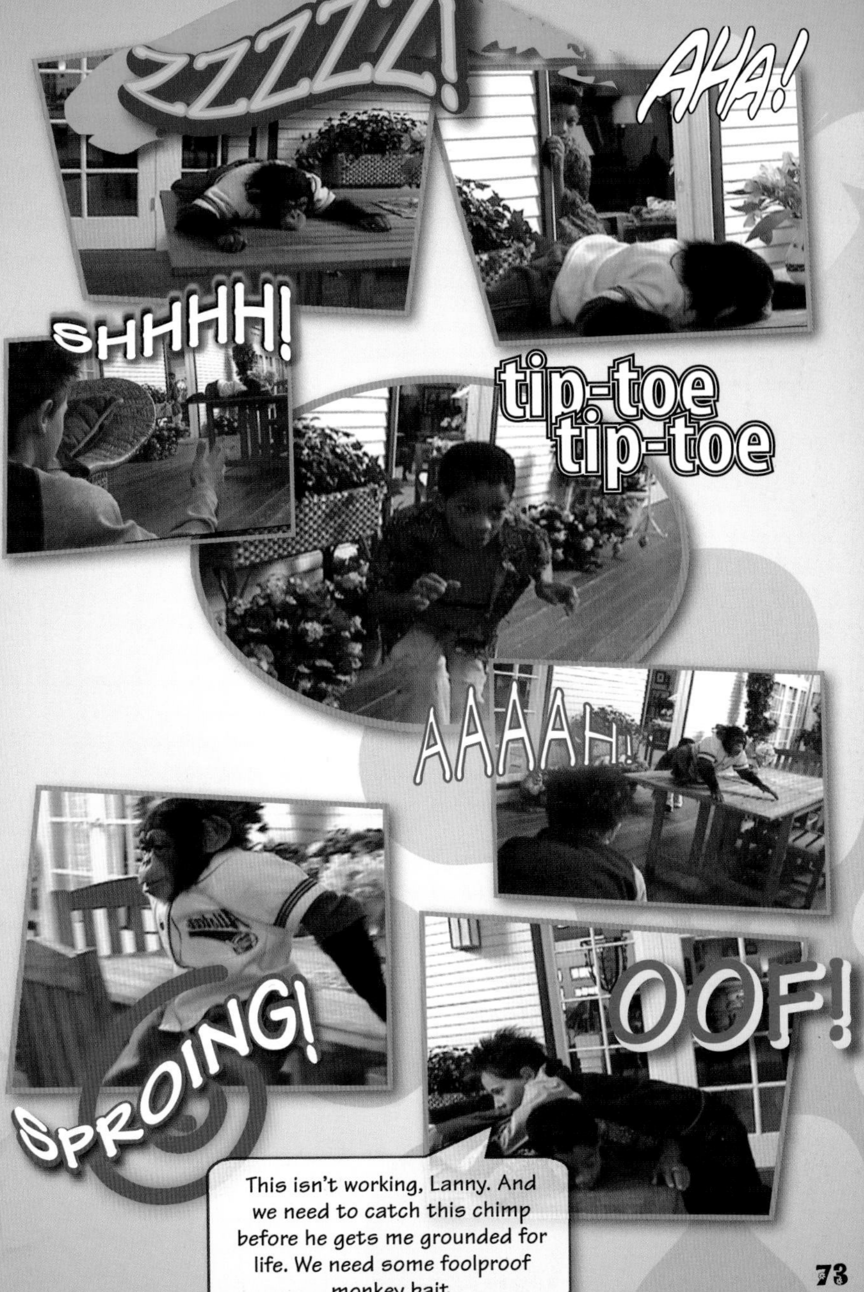
ZZZZZ!
AHA!
SHHHH!
tip-toe
tip-toe
AAAAH!
SPROING!
OOF!
This isn't working, Lanny. And we need to catch this chimp before he gets me grounded for life. We need some foolproof monkey bait.

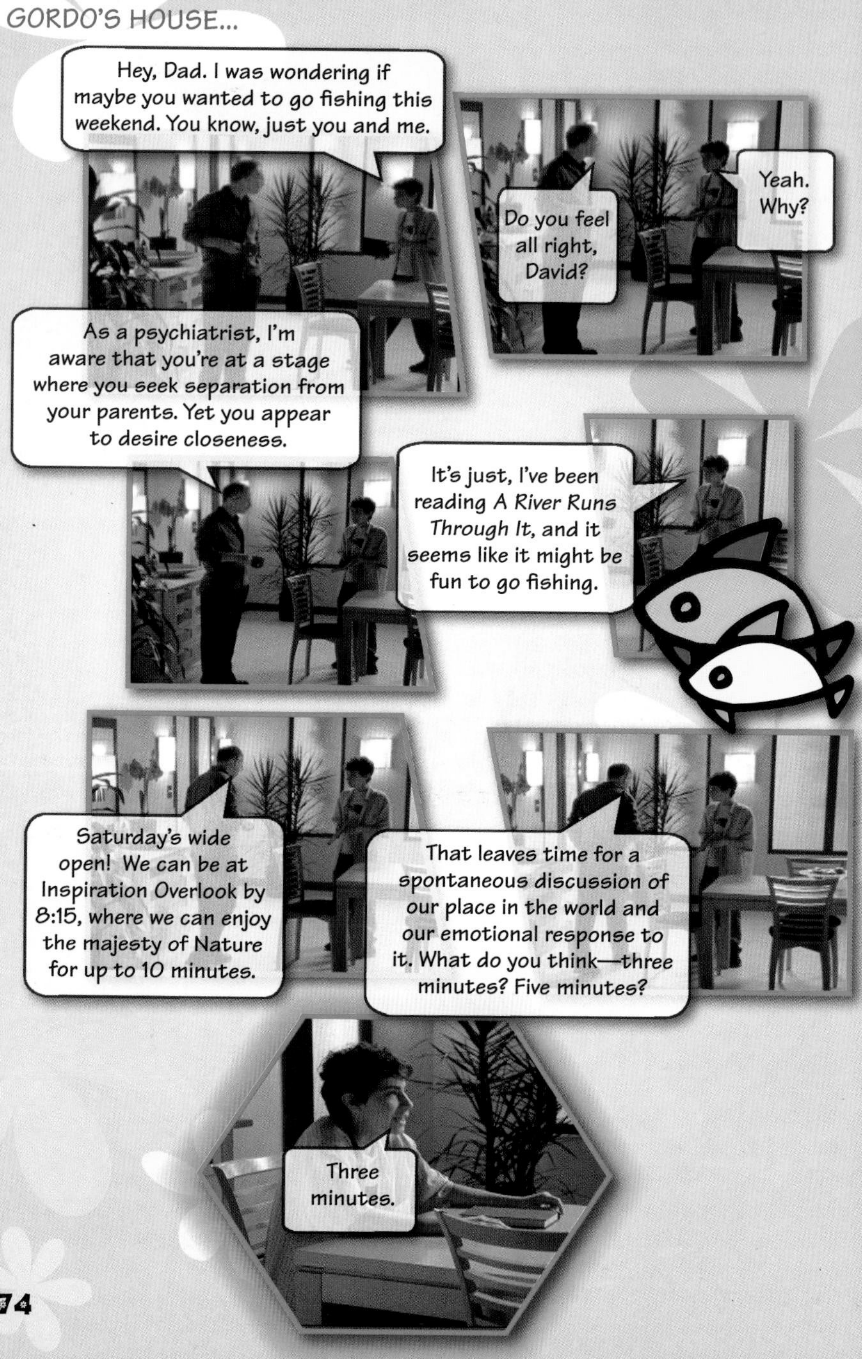
GORDO'S HOUSE...
Hey, Dad. I was wondering if maybe you wanted to go fishing this weekend. You know, just you and me.
Do you feel all right, David?
Yeah. Why?
As a psychiatrist, I'm aware that you're at a stage where you seek separation from your parents. Yet you appear to desire closeness.
It's just, I've been reading *A River Runs Through It*, and it seems like it might be fun to go fishing.
Saturday's wide open! We can be at Inspiration Overlook by 8:15, where we can enjoy the majesty of Nature for up to 10 minutes.
That leaves time for a spontaneous discussion of our place in the world and our emotional response to it. What do you think—three minutes? Five minutes?
Three minutes.

MIRANDA'S HOUSE...

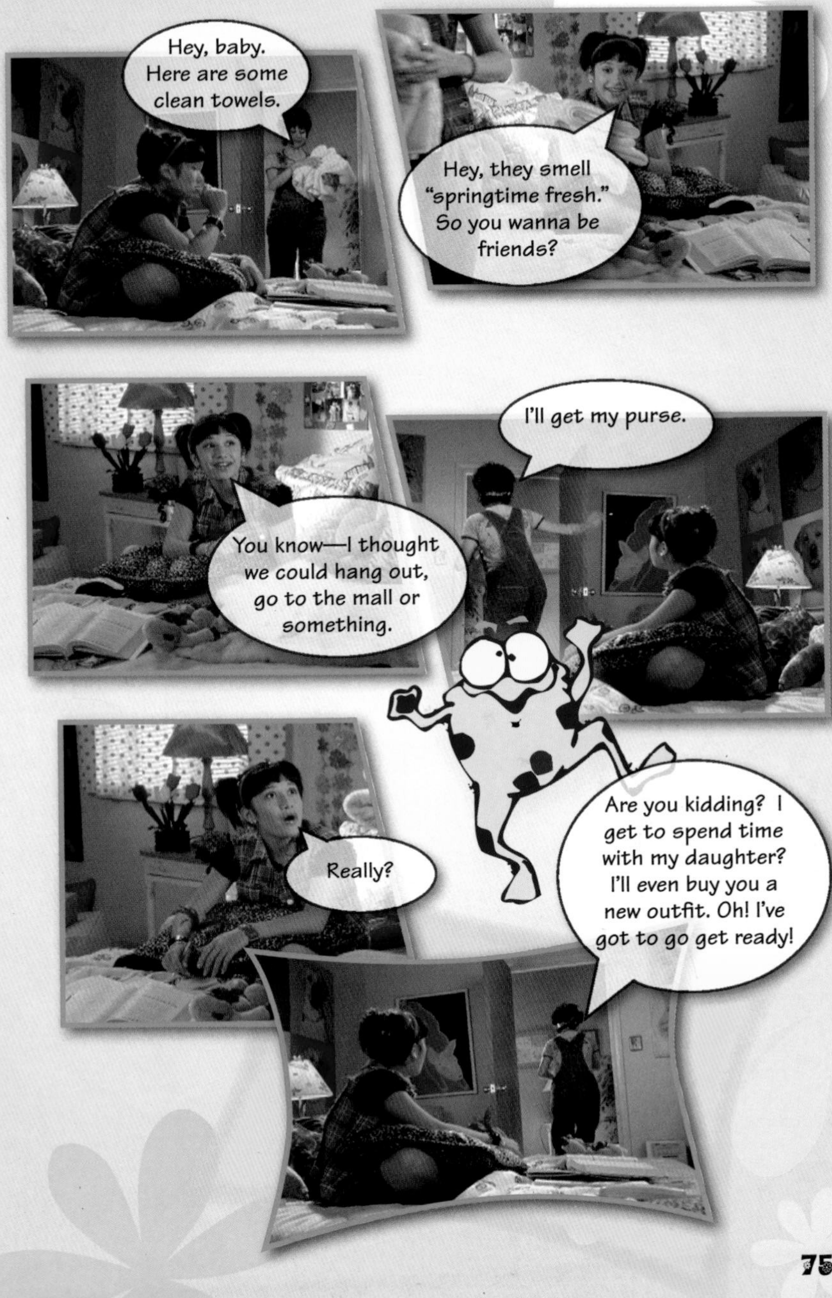
Hey, baby. Here are some clean towels.
Hey, they smell "springtime fresh." So you wanna be friends?
You know—I thought we could hang out, go to the mall or something.
I'll get my purse.
Really?
Are you kidding? I get to spend time with my daughter? I'll even buy you a new outfit. Oh! I've got to go get ready!

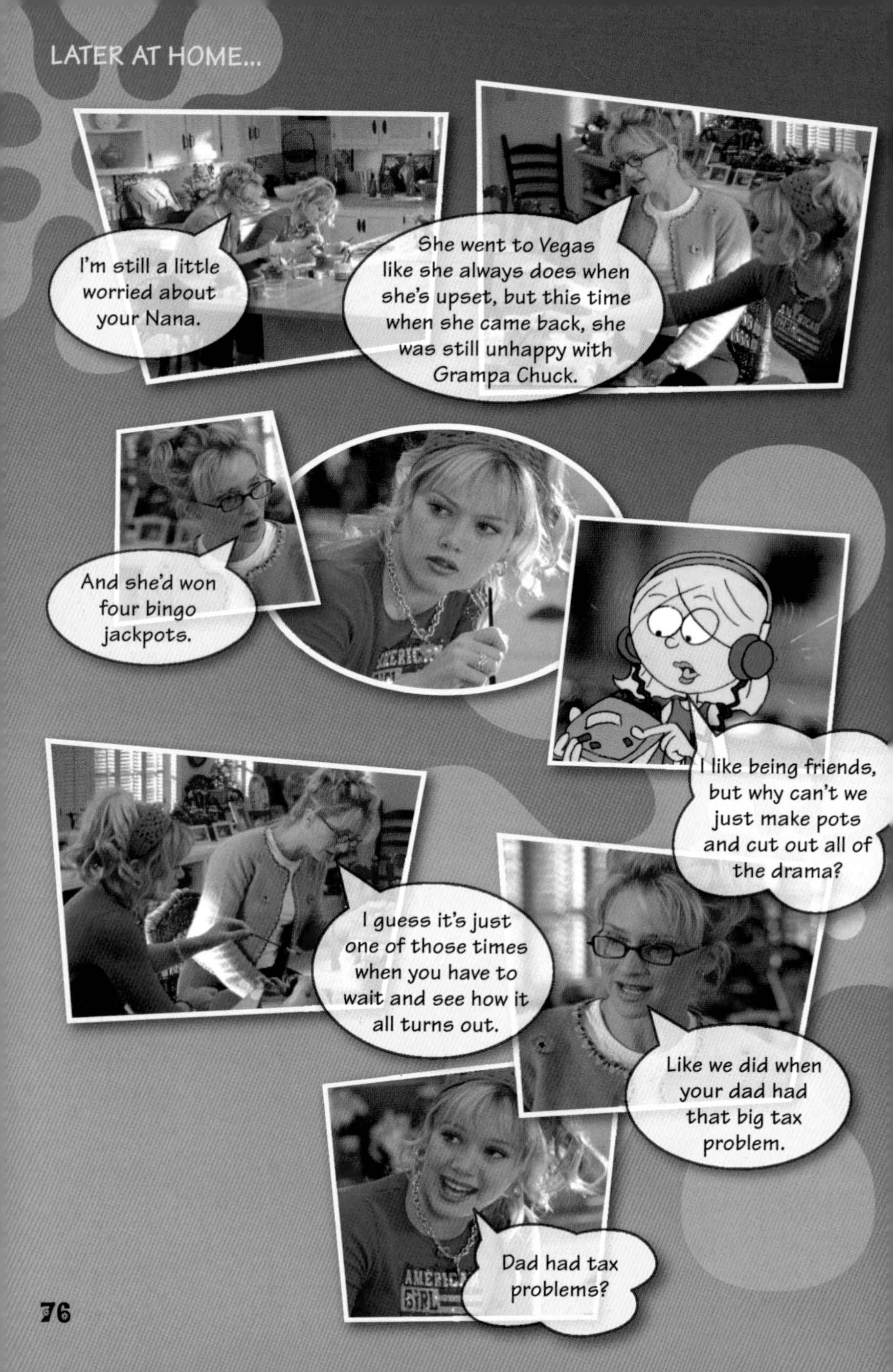
LATER AT HOME...
I'm still a little worried about your Nana.
She went to Vegas like she always does when she's upset, but this time when she came back, she was still unhappy with Grampa Chuck.
And she'd won four bingo jackpots.
I like being friends, but why can't we just make pots and cut out all of the drama?
I guess it's just one of those times when you have to wait and see how it all turns out.
Like we did when your dad had that big tax problem.
Dad had tax problems?

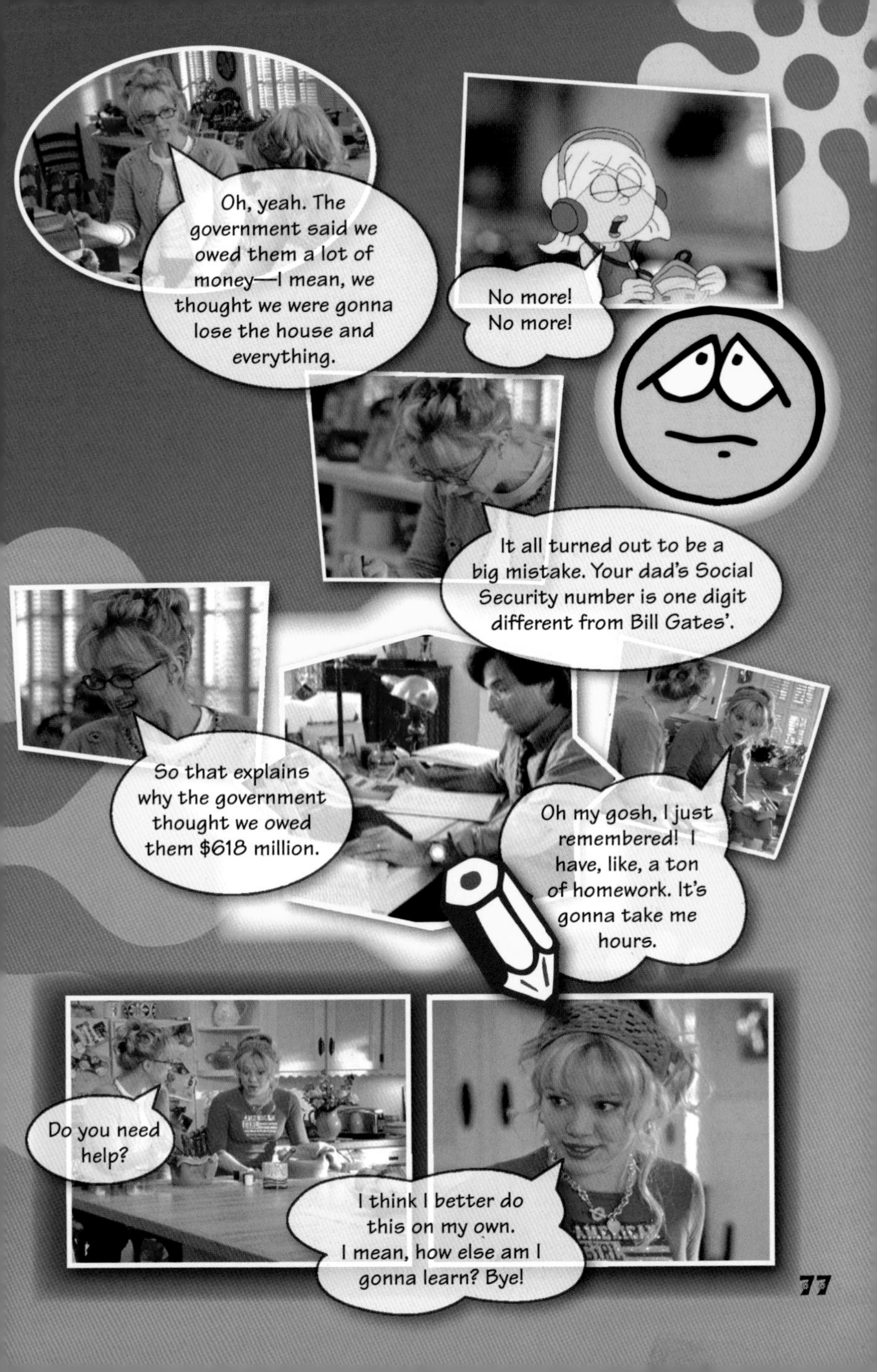
Oh, yeah. The government said we owed them a lot of money—I mean, we thought we were gonna lose the house and everything.
No more! No more!
It all turned out to be a big mistake. Your dad's Social Security number is one digit different from Bill Gates'.
So that explains why the government thought we owed them $618 million.
Oh my gosh, I just remembered! I have, like, a ton of homework. It's gonna take me hours.
Do you need help?
I think I better do this on my own. I mean, how else am I gonna learn? Bye!

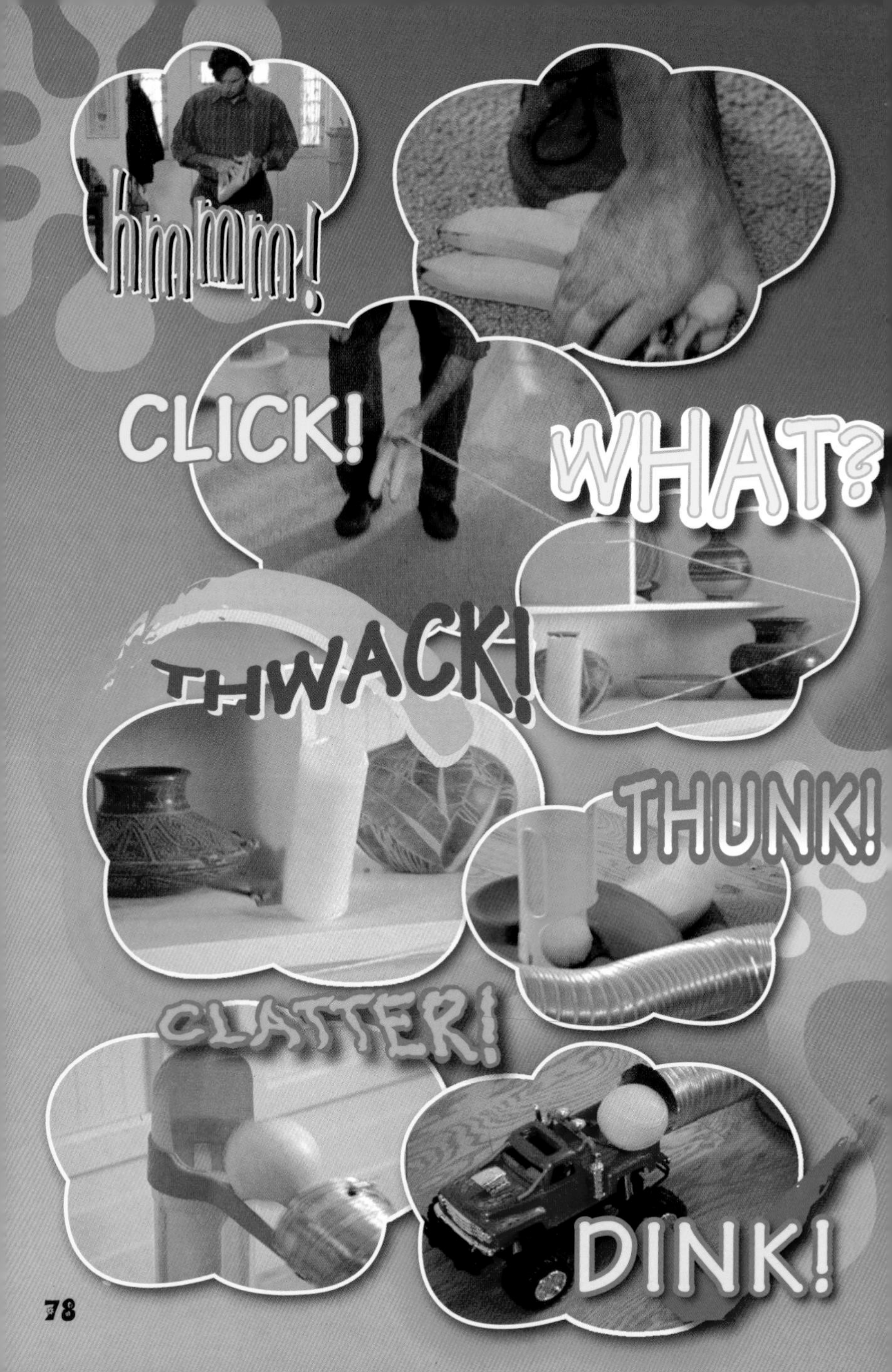
hmmm!
CLICK!
WHAT?
THWACK!
THUNK!
CLATTER!
DINK!

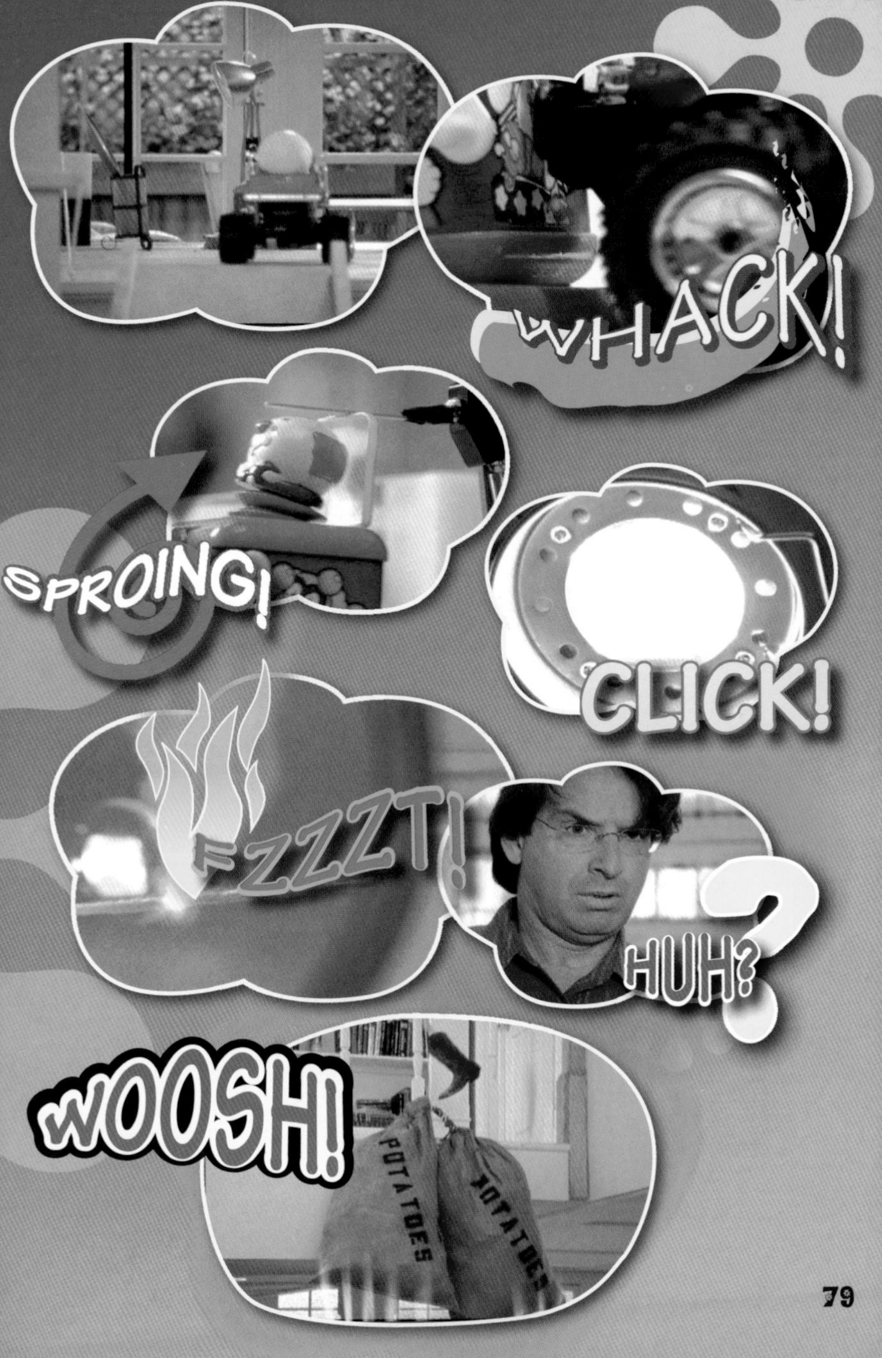
WHACK!
SPROING!
CLICK!
FZZZT!
HUH?
WOOSH!
POTATOES
POTATOES

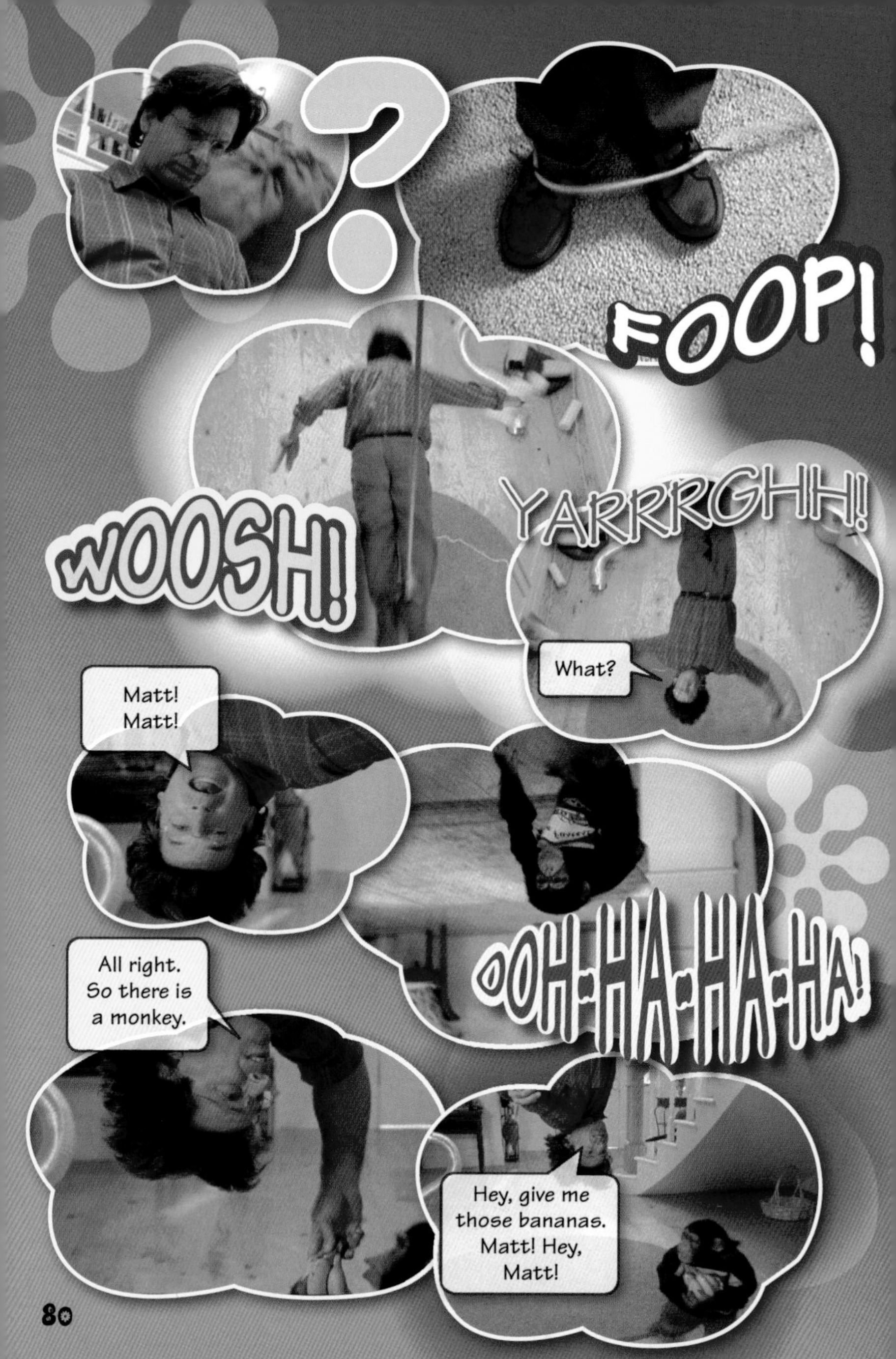
?
FOOP!
WOOSH!
YARRRGHH!
What?
Matt!
Matt!
OOH-HA-HA-HA-HA!
All right. So there is a monkey.
Hey, give me those bananas. Matt! Hey, Matt!

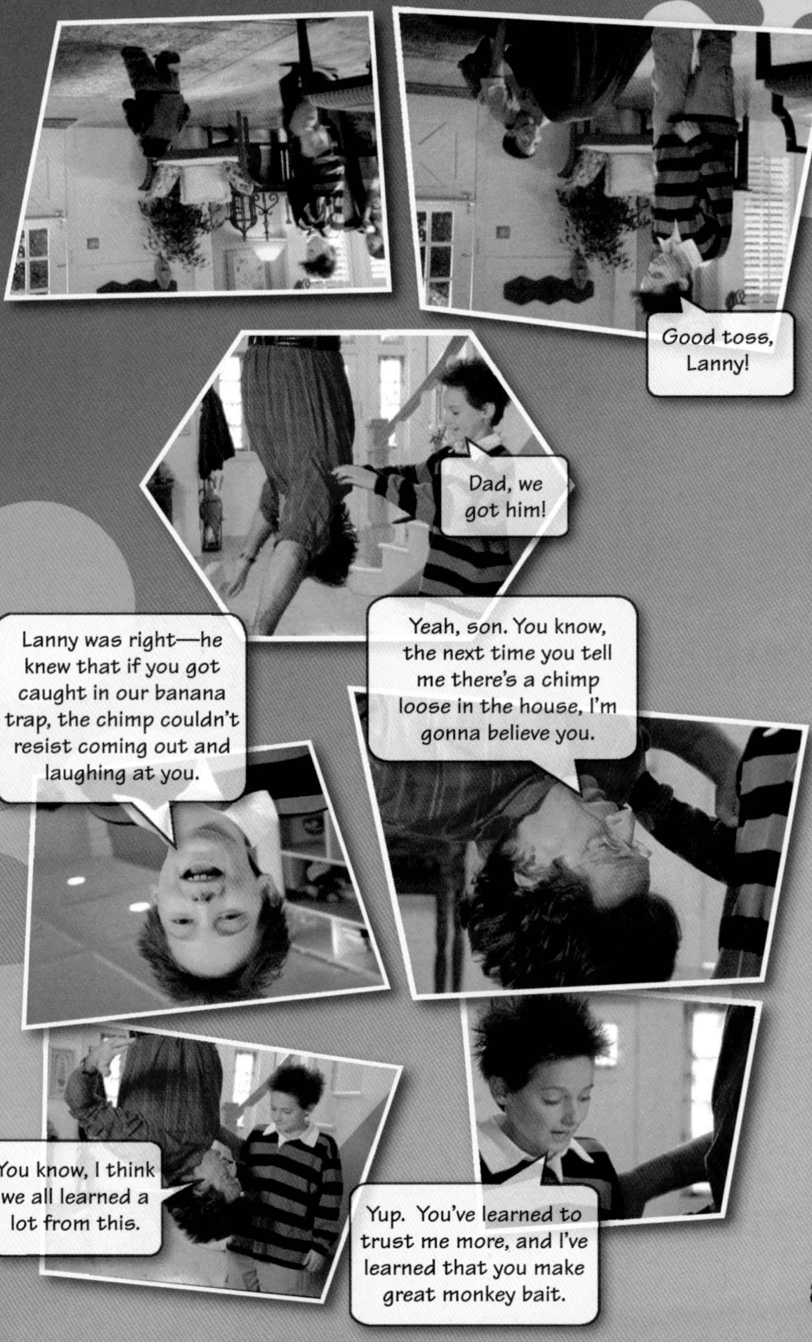
Good toss, Lanny!
Dad, we got him!
Lanny was right—he knew that if you got caught in our banana trap, the chimp couldn't resist coming out and laughing at you.
Yeah, son. You know, the next time you tell me there's a chimp loose in the house, I'm gonna believe you.
You know, I think we all learned a lot from this.
Yup. You've learned to trust me more, and I've learned that you make great monkey bait.

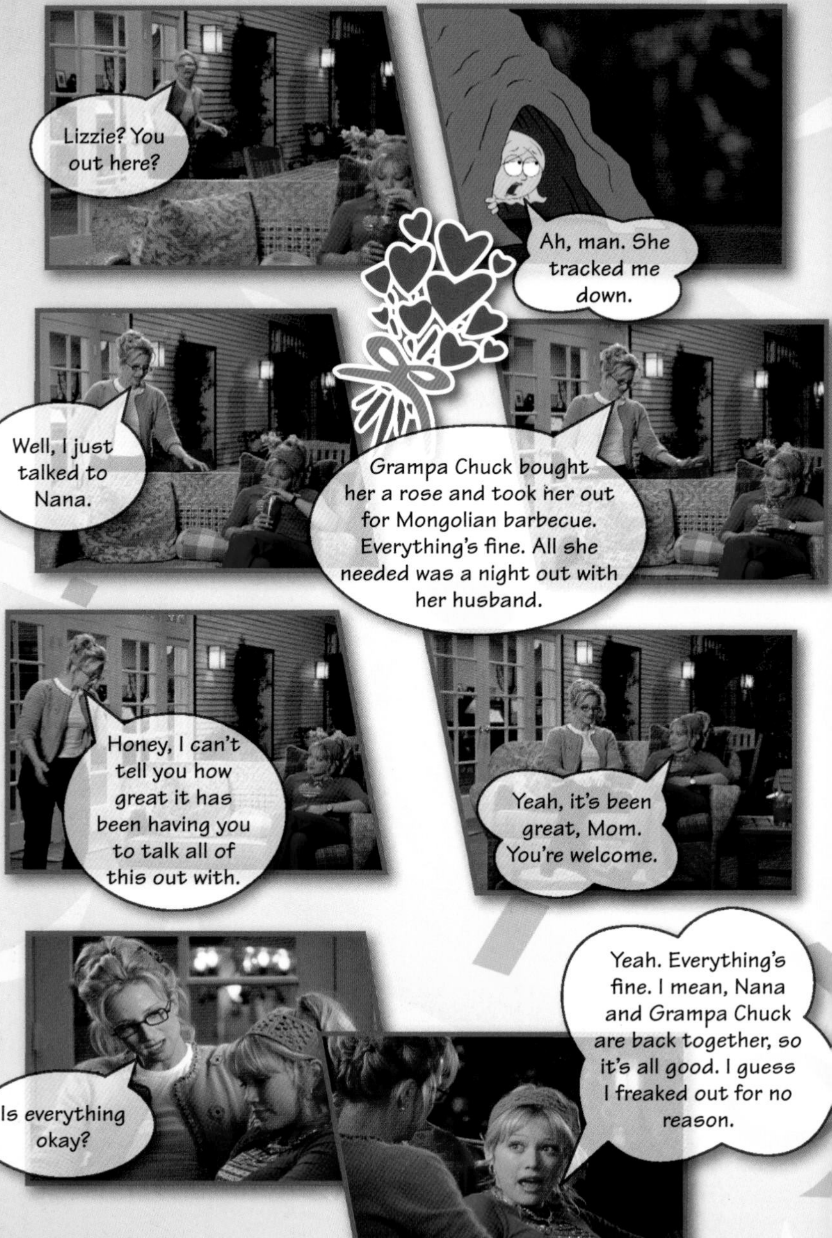
Lizzie? You out here?
Ah, man. She tracked me down.
Well, I just talked to Nana.
Grampa Chuck bought her a rose and took her out for Mongolian barbecue. Everything's fine. All she needed was a night out with her husband.
Honey, I can't tell you how great it has been having you to talk all of this out with.
Yeah, it's been great, Mom. You're welcome.
Is everything okay?
Yeah. Everything's fine. I mean, Nana and Grampa Chuck are back together, so it's all good. I guess I freaked out for no reason.

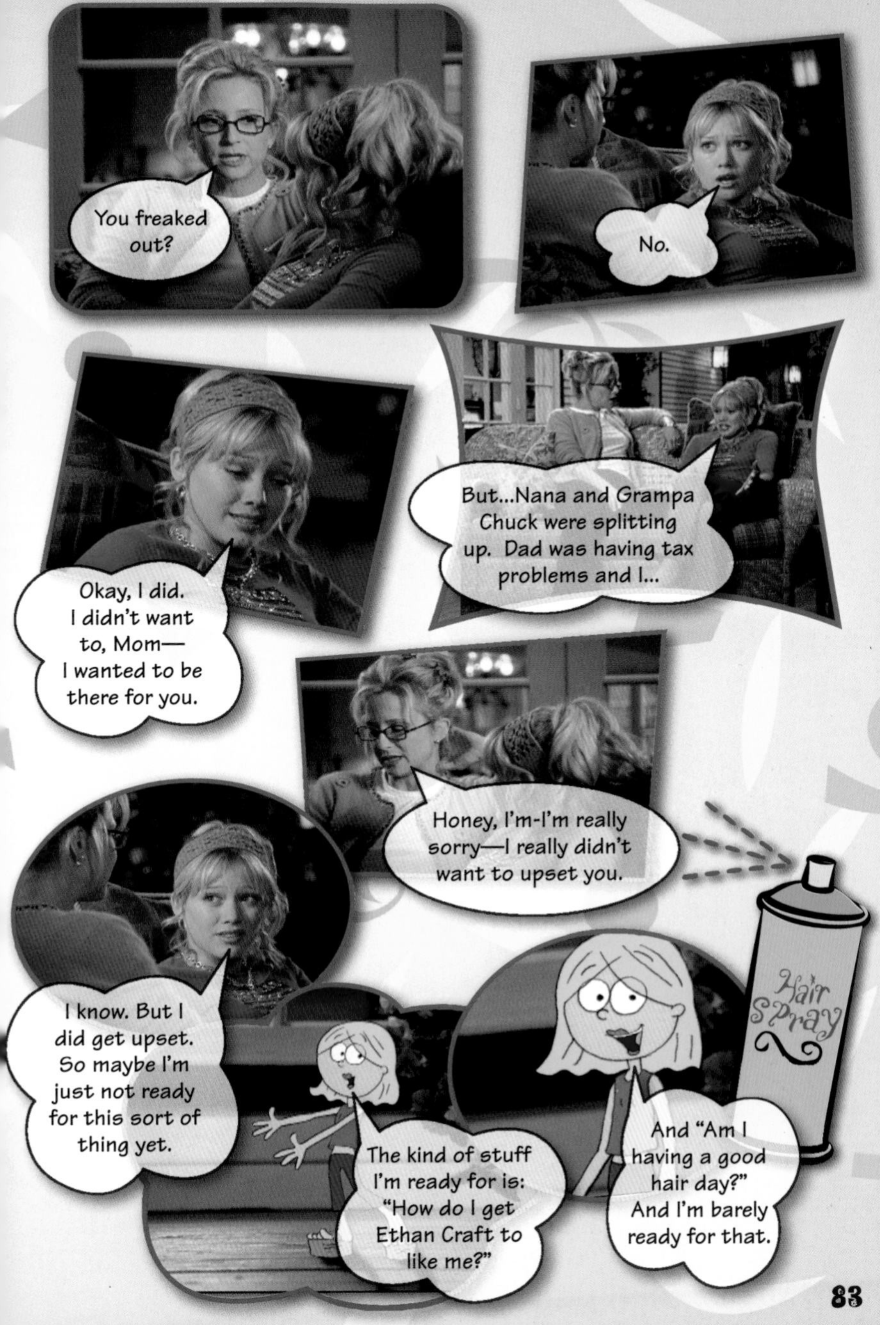
You freaked out?
No.
Okay, I did. I didn't want to, Mom— I wanted to be there for you.
But...Nana and Grampa Chuck were splitting up. Dad was having tax problems and I...
Honey, I'm-I'm really sorry—I really didn't want to upset you.
I know. But I did get upset. So maybe I'm just not ready for this sort of thing yet.
The kind of stuff I'm ready for is: "How do I get Ethan Craft to like me?"
Hair Spray
And "Am I having a good hair day?" And I'm barely ready for that.

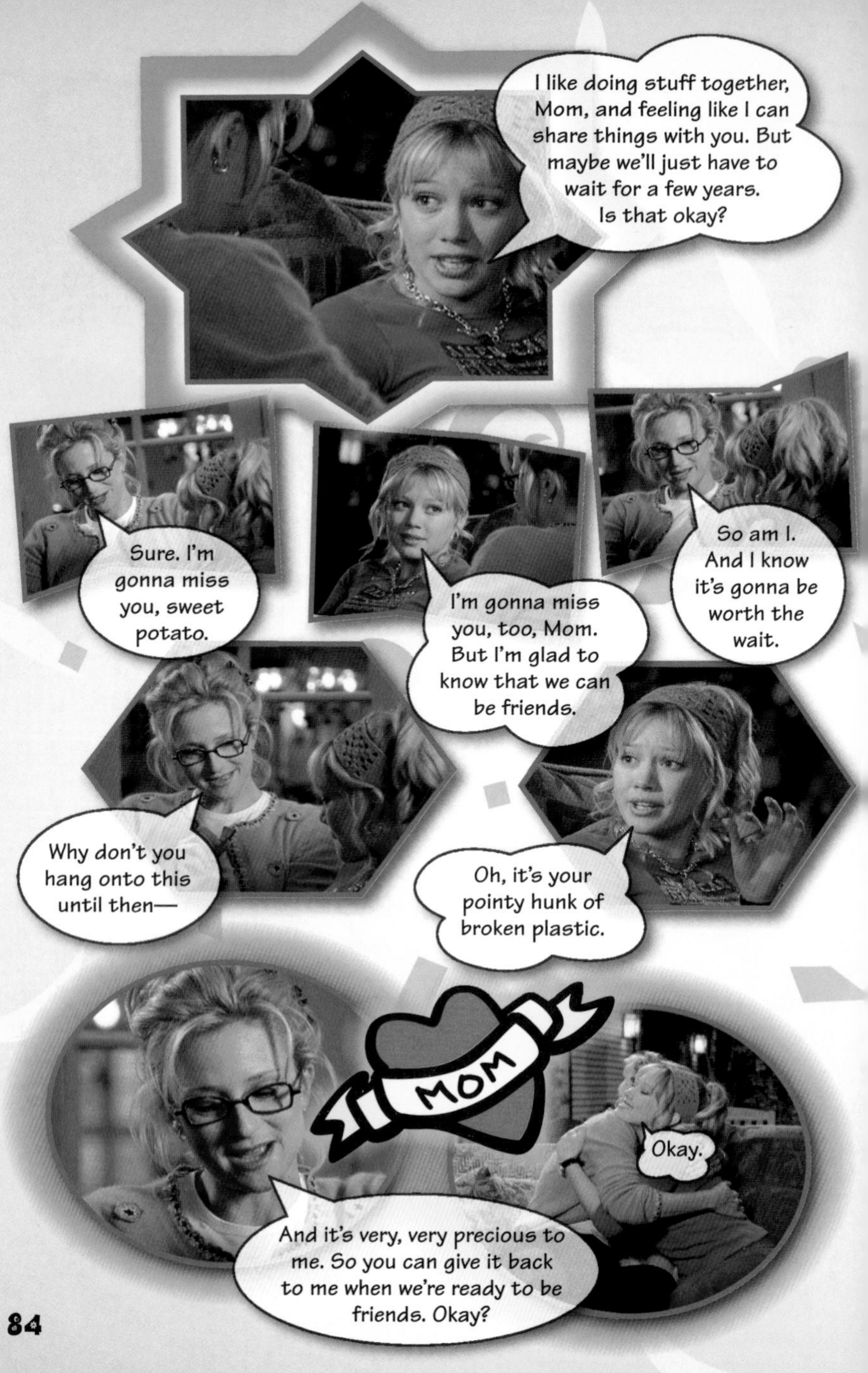
I like doing stuff together, Mom, and feeling like I can share things with you. But maybe we'll just have to wait for a few years. Is that okay?
Sure. I'm gonna miss you, sweet potato.
I'm gonna miss you, too, Mom. But I'm glad to know that we can be friends.
So am I. And I know it's gonna be worth the wait.
Why don't you hang onto this until then—
Oh, it's your pointy hunk of broken plastic.
MOM
Okay.
And it's very, very precious to me. So you can give it back to me when we're ready to be friends. Okay?

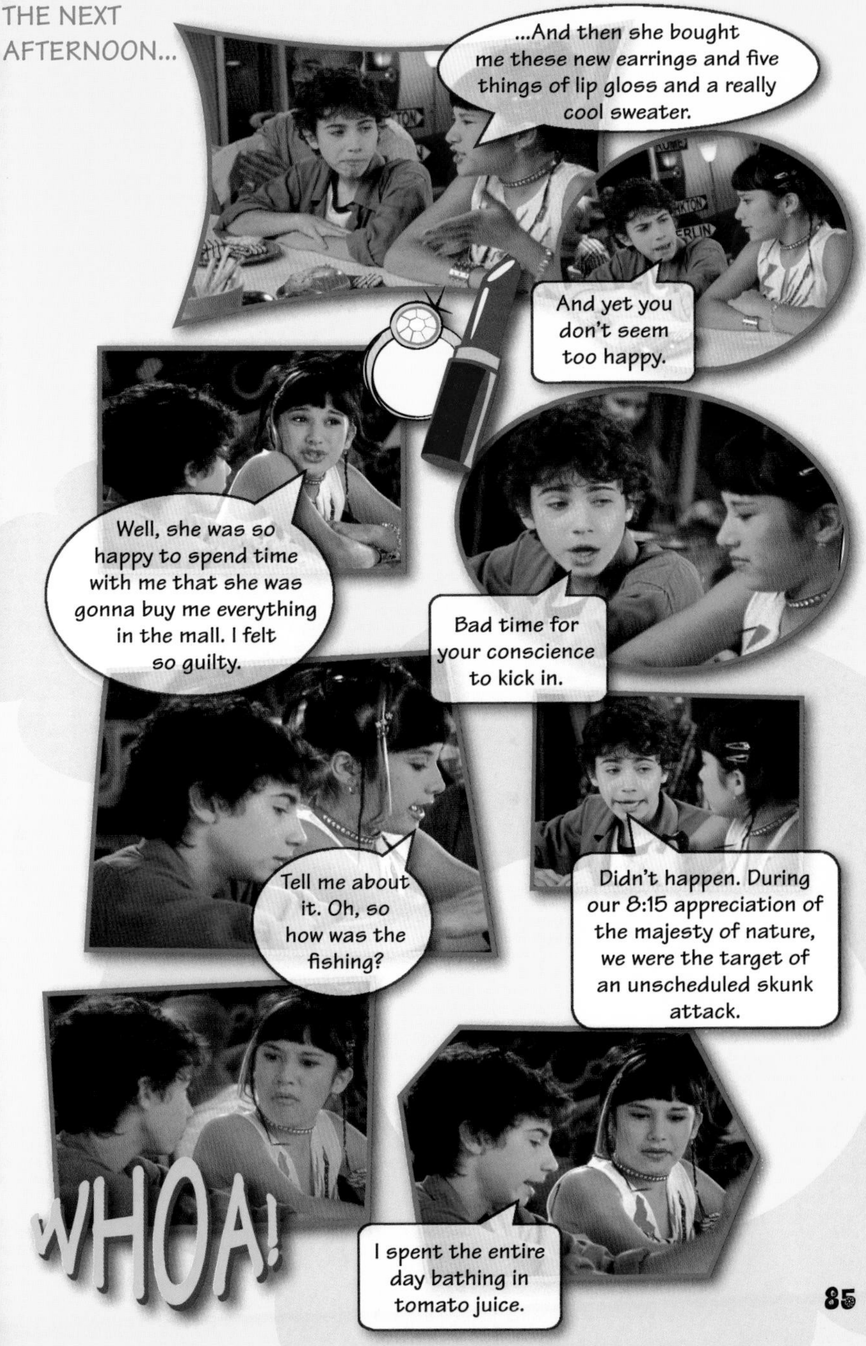
THE NEXT AFTERNOON...
...And then she bought me these new earrings and five things of lip gloss and a really cool sweater.
And yet you don't seem too happy.
Well, she was so happy to spend time with me that she was gonna buy me everything in the mall. I felt so guilty.
Bad time for your conscience to kick in.
Tell me about it. Oh, so how was the fishing?
Didn't happen. During our 8:15 appreciation of the majesty of nature, we were the target of an unscheduled skunk attack.
WHOA!
I spent the entire day bathing in tomato juice.

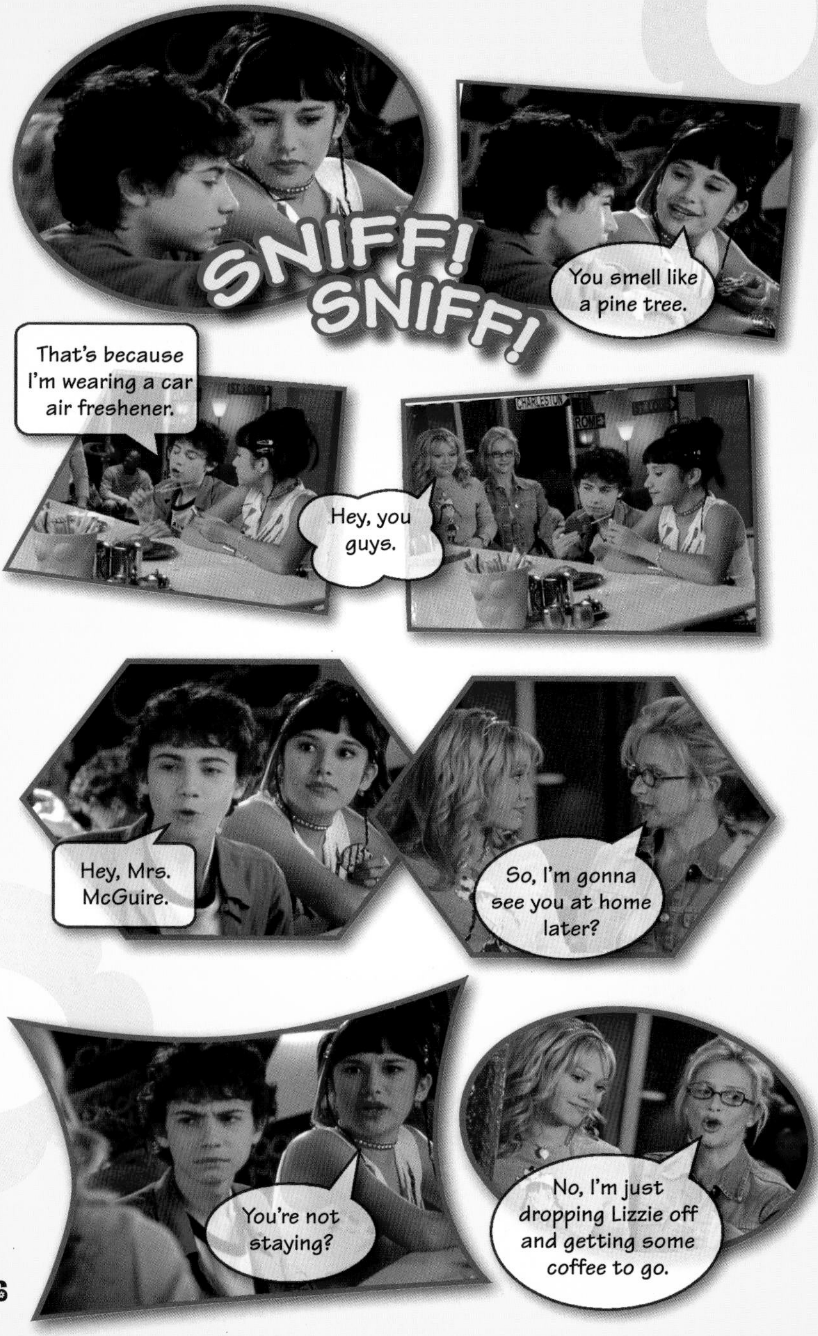
SNIFF! SNIFF!
You smell like a pine tree.
That's because I'm wearing a car air freshener.
CHARLESTON
ROME
Hey, you guys.
Hey, Mrs. McGuire.
So, I'm gonna see you at home later?
You're not staying?
No, I'm just dropping Lizzie off and getting some coffee to go.

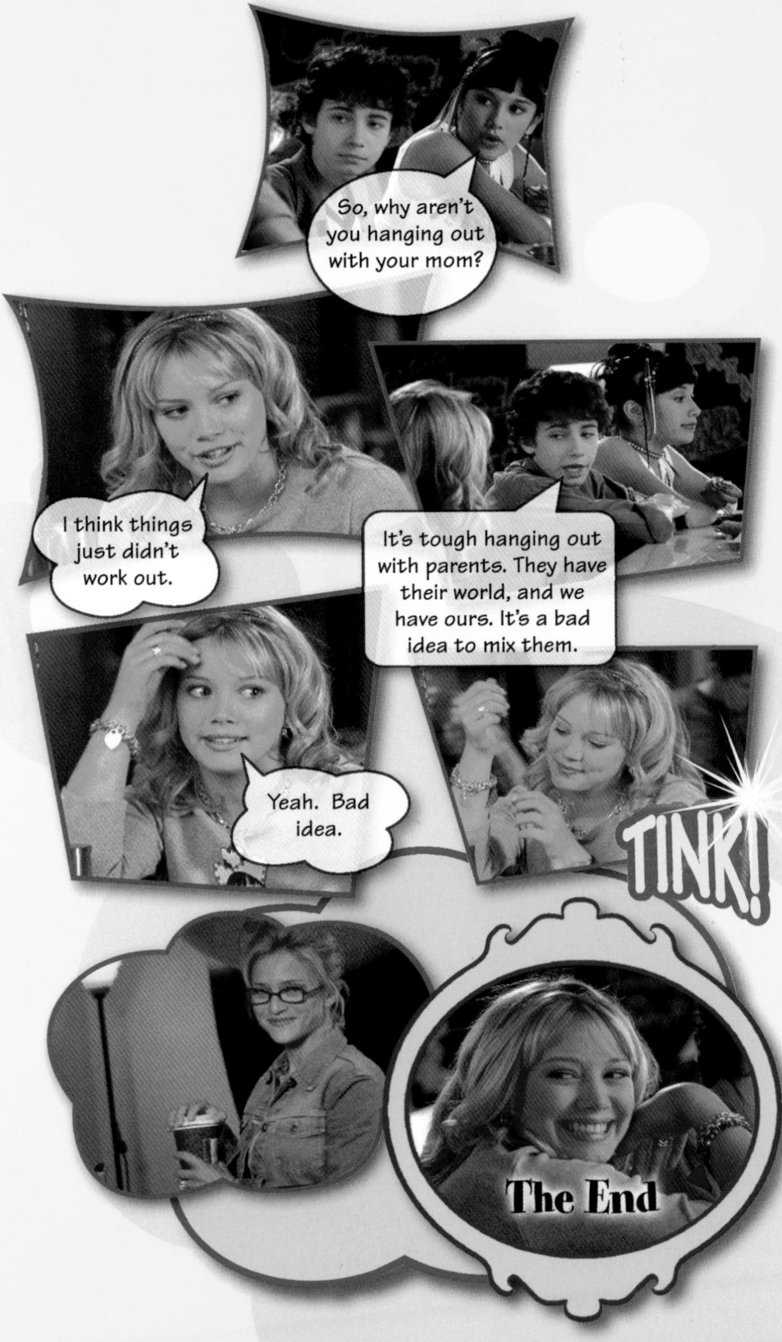
So, why aren't you hanging out with your mom?
I think things just didn't work out.
It's tough hanging out with parents. They have their world, and we have ours. It's a bad idea to mix them.
Yeah. Bad idea.
TINK!
The End

Lizzie McGUiRE

CINE-MANGA™ VOLUME 7

COMING SOON FROM TOKYOPOP®

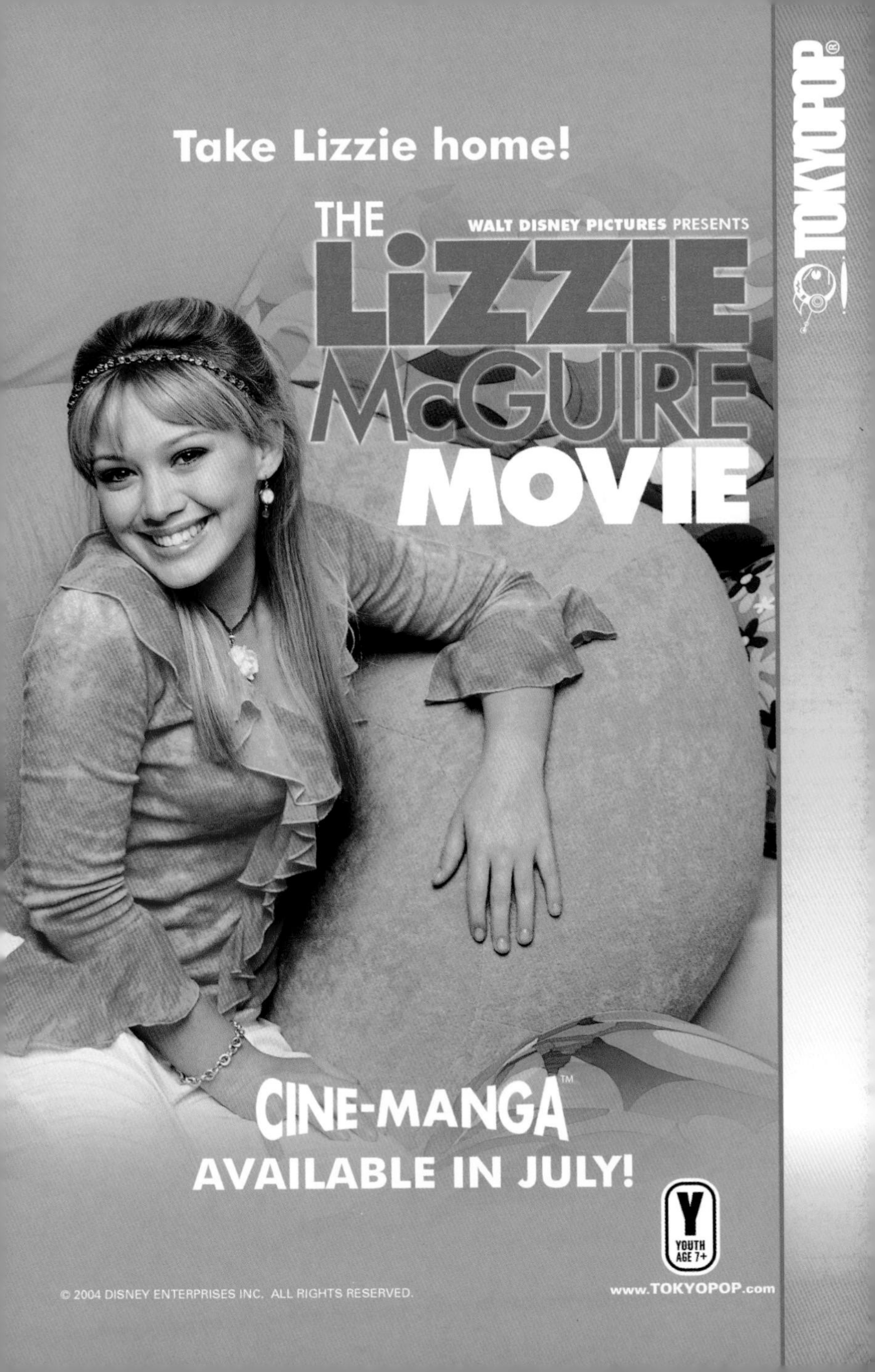

Take Lizzie home!
WALT DISNEY PICTURES PRESENTS
THE LIZZIE McGUIRE MOVIE
CINE-MANGA™
AVAILABLE IN JULY!
Y
YOUTH AGE 7+
© 2004 DISNEY ENTERPRISES INC. ALL RIGHTS RESERVED.
www.TOKYOPOP.com
TOKYOPOP®

MANGA

.HACK//LEGEND OF THE TWILIGHT
ANGELIC LAYER
BABY BIRTH
BRAIN POWERED
BRIGADOON
B'TX
CANDIDATE FOR GODDESS, THE
CARDCAPTOR SAKURA
CARDCAPTOR SAKURA - MASTER OF THE CLOW
CHRONICLES OF THE CURSED SWORD
CLAMP SCHOOL DETECTIVES
CLOVER
COMIC PARTY
CORRECTOR YUI
COWBOY BEBOP
COWBOY BEBOP: SHOOTING STAR
CRAZY LOVE STORY
CRESCENT MOON
CULDCEPT
CYBORG 009
D•N•ANGEL
DEMON DIARY
DEMON ORORON, THE
DIGIMON
DIGIMON TAMERS
DIGIMON ZERO TWO
DRAGON HUNTER
DRAGON KNIGHTS
DRAGON VOICE
DREAM SAGA
DUKLYON: CLAMP SCHOOL DEFENDERS
ET CETERA
ETERNITY
FAERIES' LANDING
FLCL
FORBIDDEN DANCE
FRUITS BASKET
G GUNDAM
GATEKEEPERS
GIRL GOT GAME
GUNDAM BLUE DESTINY
GUNDAM SEED ASTRAY
GUNDAM WING
GUNDAM WING: BATTLEFIELD OF PACIFISTS
GUNDAM WING: ENDLESS WALTZ

GUNDAM WING: THE LAST OUTPOST (G-UNIT)
HANDS OFF!
HARLEM BEAT
IMMORTAL RAIN
I.N.V.U.
INITIAL D
INSTANT TEEN: JUST ADD NUTS
JING: KING OF BANDITS
JING: KING OF BANDITS - TWILIGHT TALES
JULINE
KARE KANO
KILL ME, KISS ME
KINDAICHI CASE FILES, THE
KING OF HELL
KODOCHA: SANA'S STAGE
LEGEND OF CHUN HYANG, THE
MAGIC KNIGHT RAYEARTH I
MAGIC KNIGHT RAYEARTH II
MAN OF MANY FACES
MARMALADE BOY
MARS
MARS: HORSE WITH NO NAME
METROID
MINK
MIRACLE GIRLS
MODEL
ONE
ONE I LOVE, THE
PEACH GIRL
PEACH GIRL: CHANGE OF HEART
PITA-TEN
PLANET LADDER
PLANETES
PRINCESS AI
PSYCHIC ACADEMY
RAGNAROK
RAVE MASTER
REALITY CHECK
REBIRTH
REBOUND
RISING STARS OF MANGA
SAILOR MOON
SAINT TAIL
SAMURAI GIRL REAL BOUT HIGH SCHOOL
SEIKAI TRILOGY, THE
SGT. FROG
SHAOLIN SISTERS

03.03.04Y

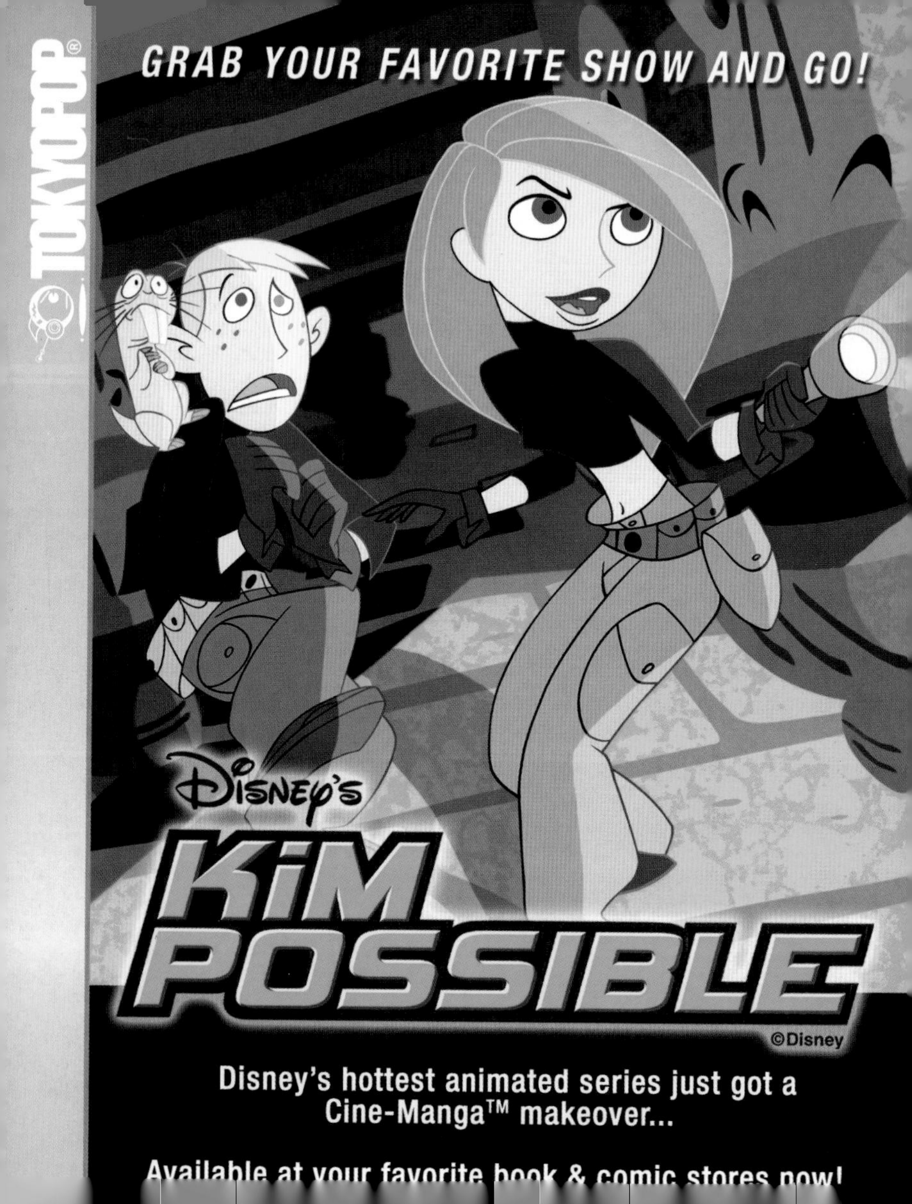
TOKYOPOP
GRAB YOUR FAVORITE SHOW AND GO!
Disney's
Kim Possible
©Disney
Disney's hottest animated series just got a Cine-Manga™ makeover...
Available at your favorite book & comic stores now!

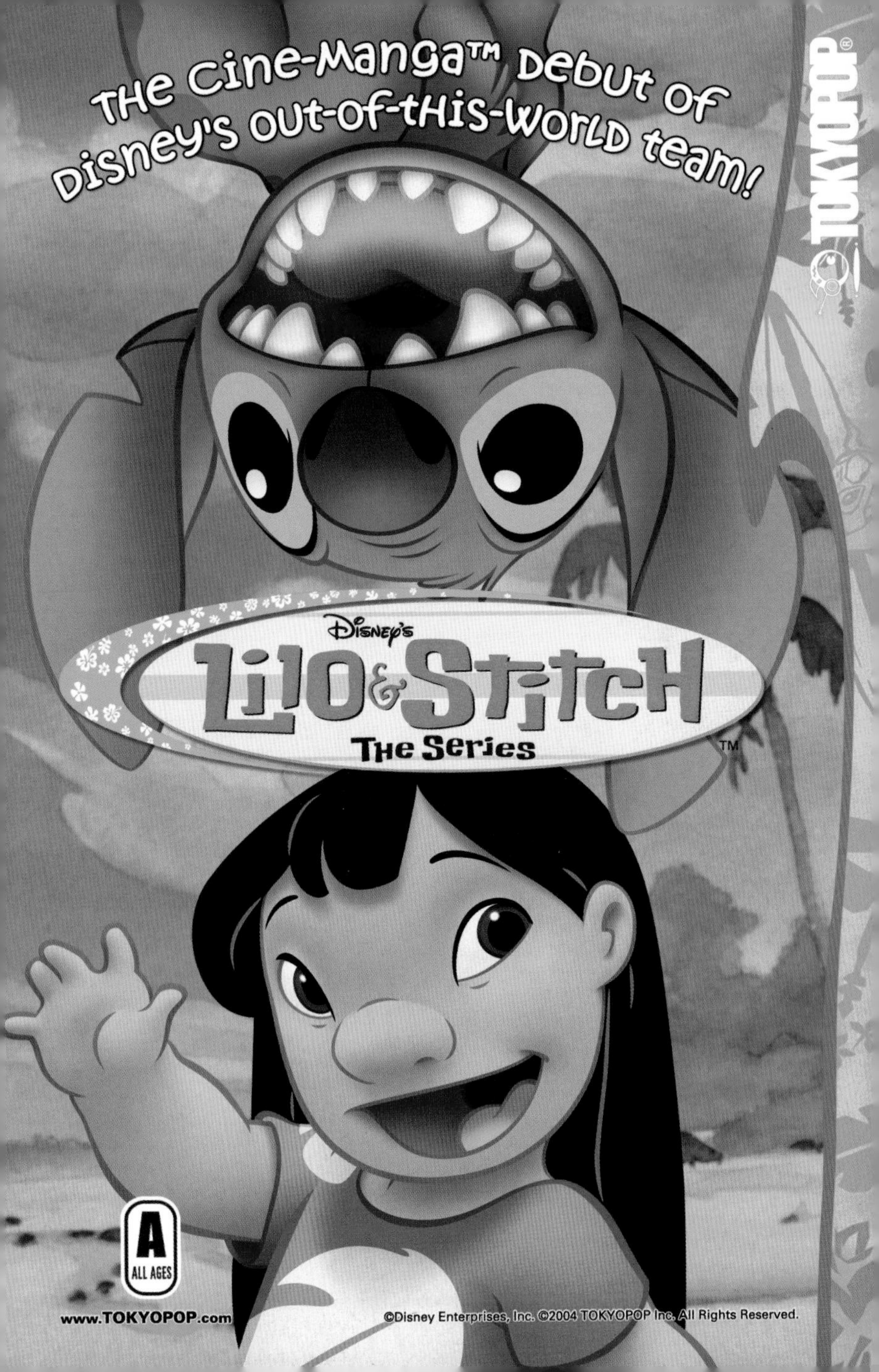
THE Cine-Manga™ Debut of
Disney's OUT-OF-tHIS-WORLD team!
TOKYOPOP®
Disney's
Lilo & Stitch
The Series
™
A
ALL AGES
www.TOKYOPOP.com
©Disney Enterprises, Inc. ©2004 TOKYOPOP Inc. All Rights Reserved.

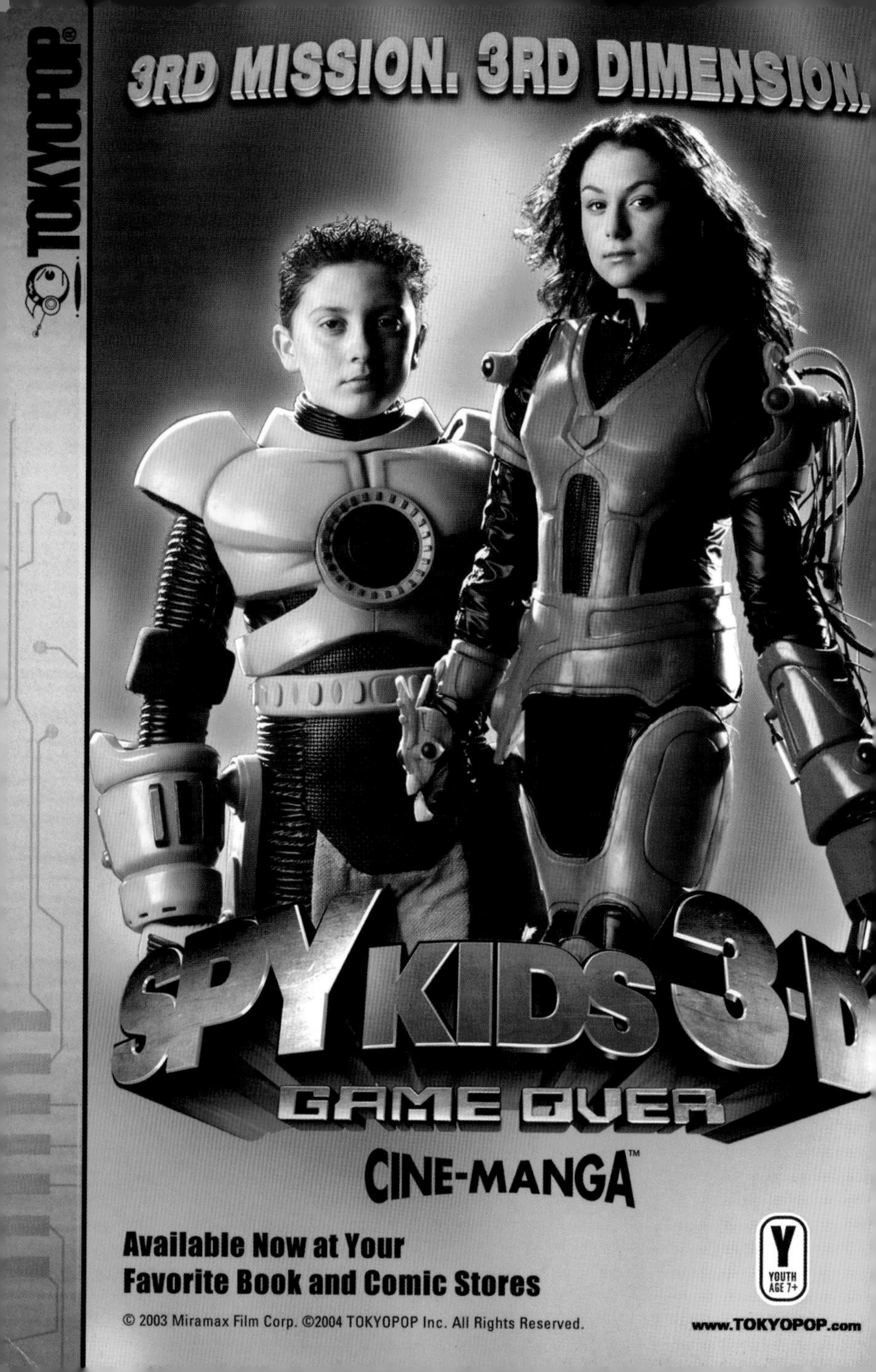
TOKYOPOP
3RD MISSION. 3RD DIMENSION.
SPY KIDS 3-D
GAME OVER
CINE-MANGA™
Available Now at Your
Favorite Book and Comic Stores
Y
YOUTH
AGE 7+
© 2003 Miramax Film Corp. ©2004 TOKYOPOP Inc. All Rights Reserved.
www.TOKYOPOP.com

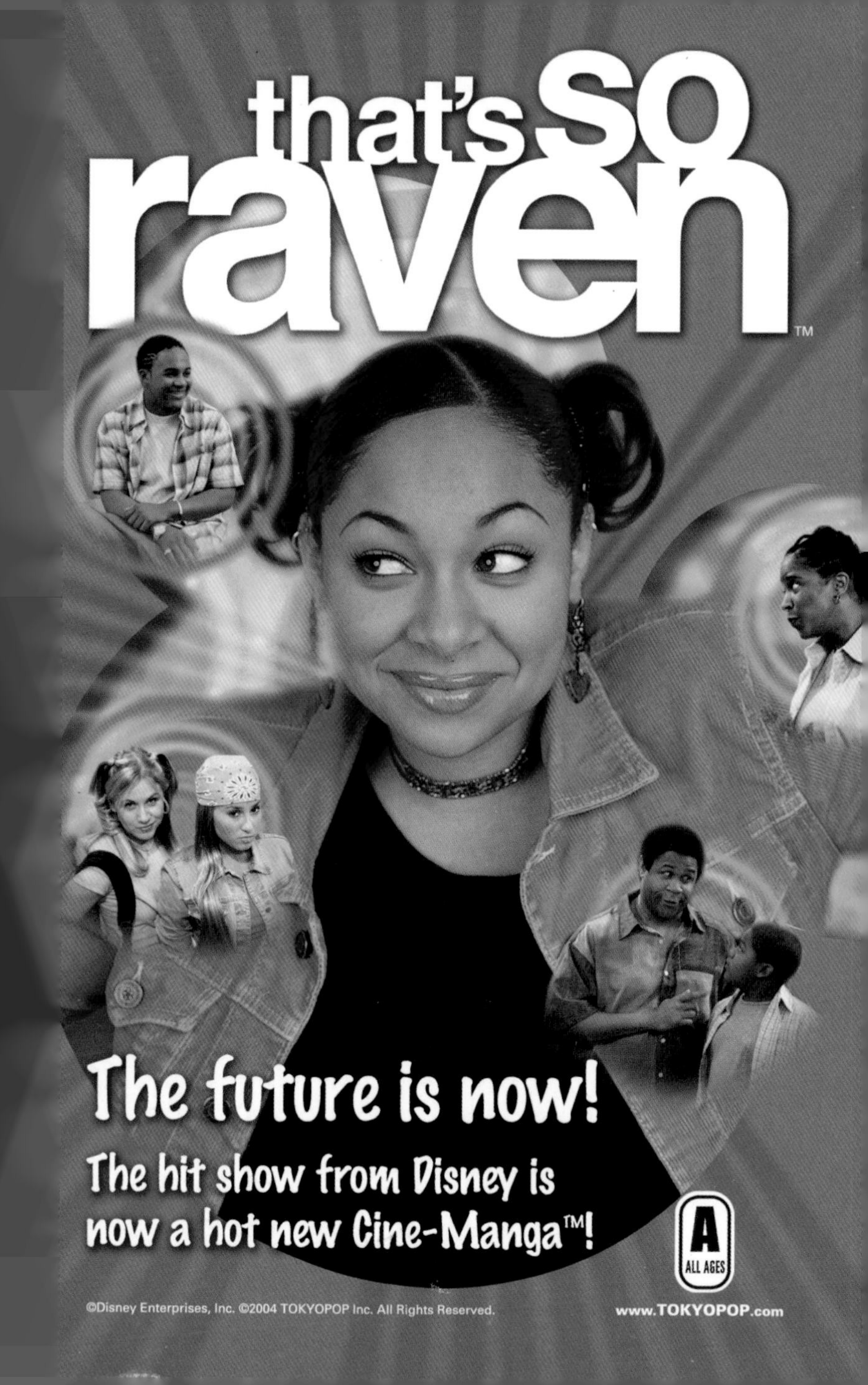
that's so raven™
The future is now!
The hit show from Disney is now a hot new Cine-Manga™!
A ALL AGES
©Disney Enterprises, Inc. ©2004 TOKYOPOP Inc. All Rights Reserved.
www.TOKYOPOP.com

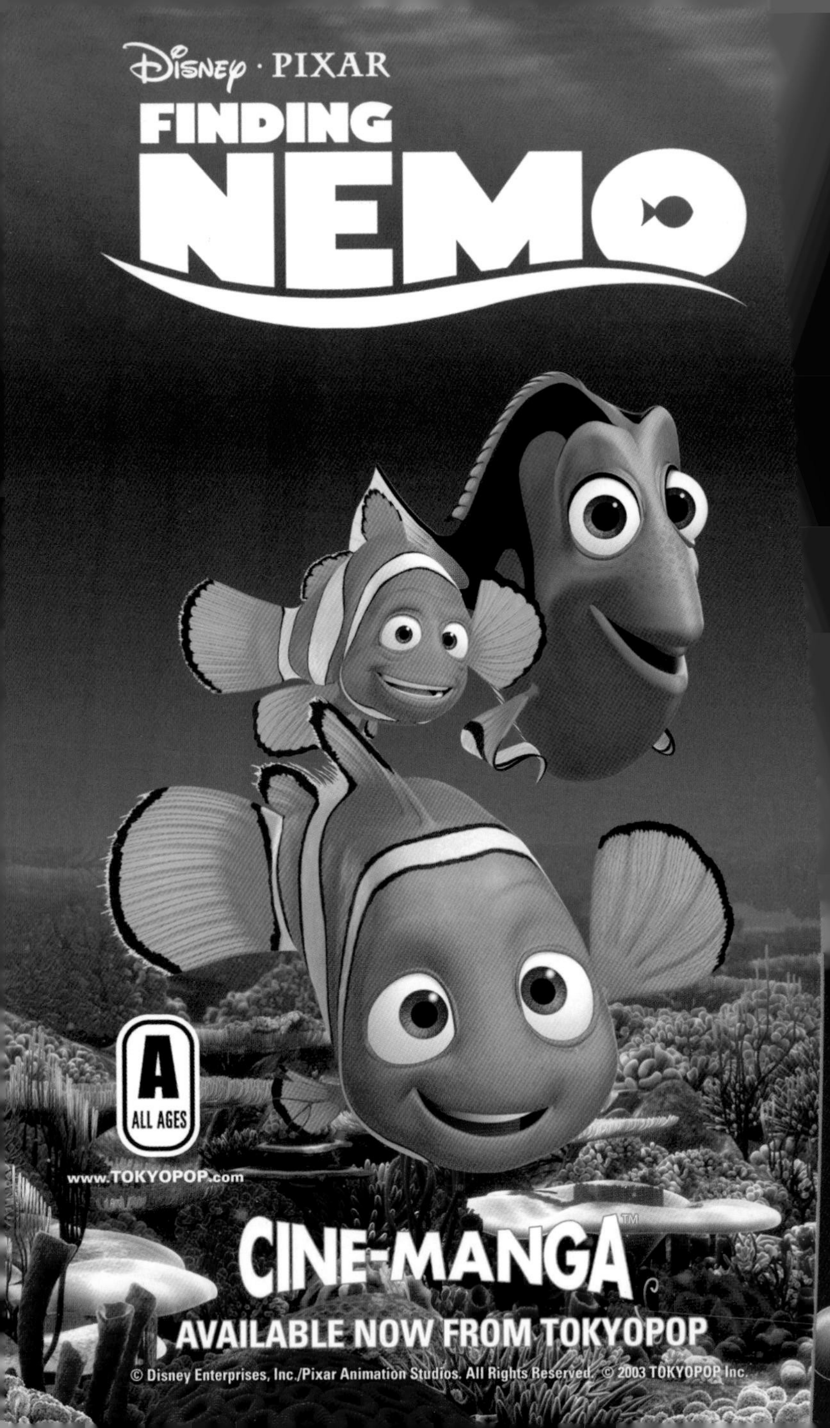
Disney · PIXAR
FINDING
NEMO
A
ALL AGES
www.TOKYOPOP.com
CINE-MANGA™
AVAILABLE NOW FROM TOKYOPOP
© Disney Enterprises, Inc./Pixar Animation Studios. All Rights Reserved. © 2003 TOKYOPOP Inc.